A WOMAN'S TOUCH

David Canning Epperson, Ph.D.

A WOMAN'S TOUCH

What Today's Women Can Teach Us About Sport & Life

Diamond Communications. Inc.
South Bend, Indiana

A WOMAN'S TOUCH
What Today's Women Can Teach Us About Sport & Life

10 9 8 7 6 5 4 3 2 1

Manufactured in the United States of America

Diamond Communications Inc.
Post Office Box 88
South Bend, Indiana 46624-0088
Orders Only: 1-800-480-3717
Fax: (219) 299-9296
Website: www.diamondbooks.com

Library of Congress Cataloging-in-Publication Data
Epperson, David Canning, 1932-
   A woman's touch : what today's women can teach us about sport
and life / by David Canning Epperson.
      p.   cm.
   ISBN 1-888698-28-4
   1. Sports—Social aspects. 2. Feminism and sports. 3. Sports for
women. I. Title.
   GV706.5 .E67 1999
   796'.082—dc21

                                                                99-30608
                                                                CIP

Contents

ACKNOWLEDGMENTS ix

PREFACE xi

PART ONE: Confessions
    1. Refusing to be a Jock 1

PART TWO: Cultural Confusion
    2. Sport, Politics, and the Greening of America 13
    3. Inside the Women's Gym: A Father's
       Surprising Discovery 31
    4. Wanted: Pretty Woman with Balls 45
    5. Journey from the Outback of Male Consciousness 55

PART THREE: Casualties
    6. The Game That Never Ends 83

PART FOUR: Creative Tension
    7. So, Do Women Hate Baseball? 93
    8. Standpoints on the Sportscape: His, Hers, and Theirs . . .111

PART FIVE: Counterpoint
    9. Sports for Tomorrow: The Culture of Counterpoint 149

EPILOGUE:
    Going for the Gold 169

REFERENCES 177

Dedicated to
Bernice Reiff Epperson
who has taught me to appreciate a woman's touch

Acknowledgments

The women in my life have been the inspiration for undertaking and completing this project. Childhood observations of the contrast between my fraternal grandmother's non-traditional "can-do" attitude and my mother's painful struggles with the limitations imposed by her Victorian upbringing, undoubtedly provoked an early interest in gender issues. My wife, and partner in women's sports administration, Bernice Reiff Epperson, has been available each day for over 50 years as an informant on the female vantage point. She and our daughters, Anna Kelley and Lara Sweeney, by becoming accomplished athletes, allowed me to share in "the joy of victory and the agony of defeat." The victories we shared were not wins on the court, for who won or lost specific matches has faded from our collective memories. But the little things we learned about ourselves as we lived our lives together, struggling to make sense out of our experiences, are indelibly recorded on the scoreboard. The loses we posted were those regular setbacks we experienced as we attempted to get people in the community to take seriously the ambitions of these dedicated athletes and their fellow competitors. The primary women in my life, along with the hundreds of young women, coaches, sports administrators, parents, and spectators with whom I have worked over the past 20 years have generously shared their thoughts and feeling with me as they were experiencing sports training and competition, either from the sidelines or on the playing field. I thank them for having encouraged me to continue to try to make sense out of my experiences with sport. And I acknowledge Pam Gill Fisher who, from my earliest years of involvement in women's sports, has urged me to persevere, even in the face of what always appear to be overwhelming odds.

I am especially grateful to two colleagues who, each in his and her own way, has led me to discover new dimensions of sport in the lives of men and women. Dr. George A. Selleck, a fellow psychologist and former Stanford teammate, has generously invested large blocks of time in reacting to my ideas, challenging me, and offering encouragement throughout this project. He has kept me on track, not allowing me to forget to make a real effort to connect with the concerns and life experiences of my readers. Mariah Burton Nelson, a writer, who is also a former Stanford athlete, has helped me understand her special vantage point on sport. Her ideas have informed my thinking about the unique challenges that sport presents for women. Both of these students of sport have contributed significantly to my understanding of the meaning of sport for men and women.

I want to express my gratitude to Ginnie Muller who offered valuable suggestions as to how to better connect with the readers.

And finally, without the encouragement, persistence, and steel-towed boot of Texan, Tom Keeling, this project would still be in the computer.

Preface

Just as women are creating a new leadership style in business,
and reintegrating the Sacred Feminine in religion, they are
changing sports by introducing caring, cooperation, and tolerance.

Patricia Aburdene and John Naisbitt
Megatrends for Women

Our daughters began their careers in sport in the late '70s when women's sports programs were just beginning to be taken seriously. While I had the opportunity to participate in college athletics in the early '50s and have been active in many aspects of sport throughout my life, it was not until our daughters got involved on their school teams that I began to seriously reflect on how sports affect the lives of those who invest in them.

I always thought I had a pretty good understanding of women's issues and took pride in my accomplishments in providing improved educational opportunities for women throughout my professional career. While I wrote my first article on the education of women nearly 35 years ago, it was not until I began supporting our daughters in their athletic careers that I came to understand just how powerful and pervasive are the forces that limit possibilities for women. During the time I worked as a volunteer administrator in girls' sports programs, while our daughters passed through the sports system from grade school through college, I was confronted each day with beliefs, attitudes, and stereotypes that keep both men and women from realizing their full potential, not only in athletics, but in every sector of their lives.

As I reflected on the frustrations I experienced with the inequities in girls' sports I started paying closer attention to how the mainstream culture of sport had affected my life and how it had limited my own ability to understand the potent role of sport in shaping both men's and women's outlooks and opportunities. While I explored further the men's and women's sports cultures, I came to appreciate just how much masculine values and traditions have been dictating how women should approach sport, and how little feminine traditions are influencing what is going on in sports for both men and women. I believe that the course that sport is currently following does not allow for the full expression of feminine possibilities that exist in both men and women. I am of the persuasion that some of the feminine qualities, if they were to receive greater emphasis, would greatly enrich the sports experiences of everyone. These feminine qualities are the same ones that are beginning to influence policies and practices in other social institutions. While it is true that women who move into non-traditional roles are being required to develop masculine qualities so that they can compete for jobs and recognition, it is also the case that the nature of present day organizations is requiring the adoption of styles of leadership and organization that reflect traditional feminine values. In short, success in today's world requires men and women to develop both strength and sensitivity.

I view the genderquake, those radical shifts in the ground upon which men and women stand, as an opportunity to reevaluate sports policies and practices. Naomi Wolf in *Fire with Fire*[1] identified the 1991 Clarence Thomas hearing as a high intensity genderquake that occurred as a result of tension that had been building up for years. From 1994 through 1999 the O.J. Simpson case seems to have been every bit as disorienting. We need to take advantage of the confusion that occurs during these shake-ups to re-assess all of our social institutions, including sport.

In this book I address the issues that have been raised by the Simpson case as well as many others that are surfacing as we consider how to adapt the institution of sport to the requirements of the times. I take the reader through the steps I experienced in coming to an understanding of the relationship between sport and gender. I then assess current trends in sports for both men and women and describe the creative tension that exists between masculine and feminine outlooks on sport. I demonstrate what a synthesis between these two approaches would look like. I continue by elaborating an alternative perspective on sport that allows for combining the best of men's and women's sports traditions. I acknowledge the virtues that men bring to sport, but conclude that women will need to be the midwives for the rebirth of this important cultural enterprise. If sports are to be in concert with the requirements of the times, if they are to be guided by principles of dignity and justice, and if they are to realize their potential of renewing the human spirit, they must be guided by feminine as well as masculine values.

As a tool for pointing up how the changing nature of gender boundaries is calling for a reevaluation of the values that govern sports policies and practices I am using a shorthand means of referring to the contrasting cultural frameworks that men and women typically bring to the sports experience. Those aspects of American culture that contribute to learning the skills, attitudes and values that prepare them to perform caretaking roles, I am referring to as the Culture of Care. Those aspects of our culture that contribute to learning how to compete in the marketplace, where competition for scarce goods and services becomes the focal point, I am referring to as the Culture of Conquest. Traditionally, Culture of Care values have been featured in the education of women, while Culture of Conquest values have dominated the education of men. There has developed what Shirley P. Burggraf in *The Feminine Economy & Economic Man*[2] refers to as "the feminine economy." This aspect of our economy has required Culture of Care skills, attitudes and values to sustain it. Likewise, the American free enterprise system has required men to learn Culture of Conquest skills, attitudes, and values so that they can effectively maintain our market system.

The feminine economy refers to "the unique functions that mostly women have traditionally performed: mothering, teaching, nursing, supporting, volunteering; in essence the caring roles as opposed to the competitive ones ..."[3] It is a system that has been the "primary producer of human capital," "the major provider in the dependency phases of the human life cycle (youth, illness, and old age)," and has "provided the human infrastructure for male workers in competitive roles." The feminine economy has brought up the young, looked after whomever needed care, and cheered on the men as they have competed in the marketplace. This aspect of the economy is characterized by its tender values. Unfortunately the feminine economy has been greatly undervalued which has contributed to the subordinate position of women in American society and hence to the subordinate role of women's sports.

In contrast, what I'll call "the masculine economy" requires

Culture of Conquest traditions to sustain it. The economic functions that men have traditionally been asked to perform are: growing crops; manufacturing, distributing, and marketing products; providing security and protection for society, and performing technical services that maintain the political, economic, and technological system. They have traditionally been the main producers of capital, primary family providers, political and economic leaders, policemen and soldiers, and major deliverers of technological services. Typically men have operated in the rough and tumble marketplace. They have been taught skills, attitudes, and values to sustain themselves in competitive environments. The aspect of the economy in which they work is often characterized by its tough values.

These masculine and feminine economies require sub-cultures and institutions, (families, schools, churches, governing bodies, media, and sport) that define the gender rules that establish how men and women should conduct themselves—how to speak, when to speak, how to walk, how to dress, what jobs to seek, who to emulate, how to protect your interests, what chores to perform at home, what subjects to like at school, what activities to value, what games to play, and how to play these games. These gender rules are defined by parental injunctions, stories we are told, rituals we enact, religious beliefs we adopt, clothes and hair styles we wear, employment we are offered, gifts we are given, rewards and recognition we receive, and sports experiences we enjoy.

I am calling for a synthesis of the masculine and feminine in sport as well as in our other social institutions, a wedding of Mars and Venus, a fusion of Culture of Conquest and Culture of Care values. I am referring to this synthesis, when it occurs, as the Culture of Counterpoint. I am inviting the reader to accompany me on my search for imaginative ways to integrate ranking and linking in the world of sport. The goal of what I am calling Connective Sports is to achieve a synthesis of questing and caring in sports policies and practices. Sport can become a common ground in the war between the sexes rather than the battleground it has sometimes become. A new generation of men and women is slowly, but surely, rejecting traditional gender boundaries. These are young people who have been infused with a vision of a gender-just world, a vision that grew out of the counter cultural revolution of the '60s. New Generation values have been shaped by the experiences of boomer parents during the cultural revolution of the Viet Nam war era and these values have been passed on to the new generation of men and women. In a variety of ways the new generation is challenging those institutional policies and practices that maintain traditional gender rules that limit the development of fully functioning men and women. The tension between old and new ways of using our social institutions is slowly but surely generating a synergy that is empowering individuals, harmonizing partnerships, enriching families, and enlivening the communities of which they are a part.

I conclude that if we wish to see principles of Connective Sports come to full fruition, a joint effort by men and women, young and old will be required. The rituals of sport can be re-scripted so that they allow for the display of both strength and sensitivity by men and women. Gender synergy, that mutual enhancement that occurs when there is a dialectic between the masculine and feminine in human affairs, can revitalize sport and enrich the lives of everyone.

This is not simply a book for athletes, past and present, or for sports enthusiasts. It is addressed to all those who are trying to achieve a better understanding of the role of sport in the lives of individuals, partnerships, families, and communities. The issues dealt with in this book are especially relevant to parents who are in the process of helping their sons and daughters determine how to relate to sport. They are also relevant to partners who are trying to determine what role sport should play in their lives together. Moms and dads coaching their son's or daughter's teams as well as career coaches can benefit from reflecting on the functions that sport performs for themselves, for their charges, and for their communities. "Football widows" as well as gym rats can enrich their lives by coming to a better understanding of sport in their lives and in the lives of their intimates. Because of the benefits that accrued to me as I reflected upon how sport had impacted the development of my masculinity, I can enthusiastically recommend that all men invest in this type of self-exploration.

Fanning and McKay in *Being a Man* conclude:

A funny thing has happened in the last thirty years. The female set of traits has risen in popularity. They have become virtues. At the same time many of the male traits have fallen into disfavor. They have become vices.[4]

Men are being challenged to make sense out of these changes.

Understanding our relationship to sport can do much to help us figure out how to respond intelligently to what is happening all around us. The investment I have made in this project has not only allowed me to come to a better understanding of the dynamics of sport in America, but also has caused me to re-examine many beliefs I have held about my role as a man—as husband, father, friend, sportsman, and citizen. My wife and I have embarked upon a belated search for ways in which we can break out of a marital script that has been in the making for over 50 years. By examining the forces at work in our family dynamic, and in our personal histories, we have been able to better understand the role sport played in shaping our relationships. Also, this soul searching has put me in touch with the ways the inner conflicts between the masculine and feminine are being played out in every sector of my life, including sport.

Sport is a very revealing arena in which to achieve an understanding of the psychological, social and cultural forces that affect the ways we think about ourselves as men and women. Since sport plays such a prominent role in American culture, neither men nor women can move through their lives without being affected, either directly or indirectly, by the ways sport is used to define gender boundaries. Since all men and women are being bombarded with competing messages about how they should establish their manhood or womanhood, it is important for all of us to develop a framework for understanding how sport is impacting our definitions of ourselves.

Many factors need to be considered in order to make sense out of these competing messages. Only when we "witness to each other, tell our stories, and listen quietly"[5] will we be able to arrive at policies and practices that allow both men and women to discover new possibilities through their experiences with sport. Mutual respect will allow us to transform a battleground into a common ground. When a common ground has been found, we will be prepared to survive the next genderquake. We will be able to intelligently and enthusiastically participate in the creation of empowering and enlivening shared experiences, on and off the playing field. Through our experiences together we can create new visions of manhood and womanhood.

The most hopeful thing we can do to end the war between the sexes is merely to witness to each other, tell our stories, and listen quietly.

Sam Keen

..... get out of the fence building business, and get into the bridge building business

Horace Deets

Confessions

CHAPTER ONE

Refusing to be a Jock

*It is so important to be macho today. It's overwhelming. A man
needs to be able to cry, to talk about feelings, to look at a
beautiful sunset, to be a person who loves poetry and nature,
and not just talk about scoring and touchdowns and home runs.*

> Dottie Belman
> Mother of a Lakewood High School (CA) athlete
> who was playing games of sexual exploitation
> with the notorious "Spur Posse."

My wife and I shared the view that sport could be
a significant arena for our daughters to develop the confidence,
courage, and resiliency required to pursue whatever life course they
chose. In the late '60's when our girls were old enough to learn some
basic motor skills, we were inspired by the "cultural revolution" to
cart them off to the Y' for classes in swimming, dancing, gymnastics,
and ice skating. We felt that it was the politically correct thing to do
to offer young girls the same opportunities that have traditionally been
provided boys. Later when our girls chose to join softball, basketball,
track, and volleyball teams, we threw ourselves into supporting this
natural extension of their athletic interests. We speculated that this
would be one way they could develop qualities that would allow them
to be unencumbered by traditional sex role limitations. We wanted
them to enjoy opportunities that were not offered their mother.

At that time, it seemed so simple. Now we better understand what
a challenge it is for parents who want their daughters to be able to
pursue any goals their talents dictate. Growing up a women in this
era, without question, is confusing, and being a parent of young
women is a significant challenge if one seeks to provide today's girls
with options that were not open to previous generations.

My experiences as a father over the past 32 years have been the
inspiration for undertaking this study of sport in the lives of the New
Generation. I have been privileged to be a participant-observer in one

of the most interesting and rapidly changing periods in human history. By being positioned squarely in the middle of the women's sports movement, where I have been able to observe the events at close range, has provided me with a front-row seat. From that vantage point I have not only witnessed victories and beautiful athletic moments but also injustice, casualties, and far too many ugly turns of events. Having been a long-time student of women's issues, I have felt privileged to be able to be in the trenches with the women in my life to witness the struggle from close range. It has been like being a war correspondent assigned to a combat unit where your own wife and children are completing tours of duty. Under these circumstances I have experienced many moments when I worried that the most important women in my life would be victimized by their sports experiences. This, of course, is what men in my era were trained for as we grew up. We clearly understood that it was our responsibility to protect the women and children in our lives. More than a few times I have felt the urge to move my wife and daughters out of harms way, to drop my note pad and camera, and pick up a weapon. We are now in a period, however, when it is in the best interest of women if the men in their lives allow them to look after themselves. We should help them develop the skills to protect themselves, but then step aside and give them a chance to show their stuff. In a way, I suspect writing this book is one of those moments when I have crawled into the trenches to share the battle with them. The weapon I have chosen is that of a pen. I have learned that when I am manning a battle station I am frequently uplifted, not only by the insights I am gaining about the challenges women face, but also by the discoveries I am making about myself and my own experiences as a male. It is not an act of altruism to join in the fray, but instead an opportunity for self-realization.

I am inviting the reader to join with me in the search for ways in which we can provide young men and women with sports experiences that allow them to develop possibilities that are not limited by whether they happen to be male or female. I am convinced if one invests in reassessing the potential of sport in the lives of both men and women, the yields will be high. Not only will the young people who participate in sport be empowered by newly fashioned sports experiences, but those of us who invest in overseeing athletic programs—coaches, referees, sports administrators, sports reporters, and parents—will discover new possibilities within ourselves as well as in the sports enterprise.

There are numerous issues that need to be attended to as we attempt to make sense out of what it means to be a man or a woman at this point in history. There are many fascinating but troubling issues that cause us to re-evaluate how we should be living our lives. Fortunately I have had exceptionally able guides to lead me through my "curriculum" of enlightenment about sport and gender. My wife, Bernice Reiff Epperson, has been called upon daily to help me make sense of my experiences with her, our daughters and the other women who are a part of our lives. She has always been a non-traditional woman. From the days of her childhood in a German-American rural family where she was expected to drive tractors, bail hay, feed calves, cook for a harvest crew, and sew her own clothes, to the days in the early '50s when she was one of only two women in the accounting curriculum at Berkeley, she has always assumed that there were no gender barriers that she could not figure out how to slip through.

When our daughters came along, they served as her "assistants" in briefing me about how women experience the boundaries in their lives. While I can never really know what it is like to experience the indignities women encounter, I have paid close attention to the intimate front-line reports I regularly receive.

One of the most important lessons I have learned while listening to the many men and women who have passed through my life is that not very many of us have the confidence or courage to free ourselves from traditional sex role constraints. This is especially true for the vast majority of men and women who choose to participate in sport. They and their families may hope that sports experiences will allow them to broaden the range of options open to them, but they are, in the main, conservative souls who are reluctant to take the risks necessary to effect change in their lives. Traditional feminine passivity and dependency are difficult for many young women to abandon, even those bold enough to pursue athletic careers. And traditional male privileges give few of us, especially athletes, the incentive to change our ways. While our culture has given birth to both Madonna and Mr. Rogers, at this point very few have chosen to become tough women or tender men. It is good news that women are reluctant to give up their tender feminine ways. It is also encouraging to know that nearly two generations of men have been exposed to the male model Fred Rogers projects to young viewers.

Most women endow the sports environment with a wonderful

caring ethos which serves to counter the sometimes brutish aspects of male-led mainstream sports. This book is about the qualities I have discovered in both the men's and women's sports cultures that deserve to be amplified and incorporated into sports policies and practices for a New Generation. It is also about those traditional cultural patterns that might be better left at the gym door. We men would not have been provoked to re-examine our perspective on sport if it were not for the women in our lives who have caused us to re-think how we have been conducting ourselves both in and out of the gym. Without a doubt, women, with firm but gentle voices, are inviting us to re-assess, not only how we compete on the playing field, but also how we play the game of life. All of us men can benefit by listening. Also, women's sports provide powerful settings in which women can benefit from paying attention to male sports traditions. Men and women are, indeed, different. We need to continue the search for ways to use these differences to enrich our lives together.

This book is about how new opportunities for personal growth can be discovered by men and women as they attempt to work out their relationships to the world of sport. Since sport has traditionally been considered a primary vehicle for teaching men those qualities of toughness required for success in the "real world," it is impossible to ignore sport in any serious discussion about the redefinition of gender boundaries. As we enter a new era in American life we are coming to understand that the requirements for successfully meeting the challenges of the day demand a different approach than has been used in past eras.

Who then can be looked to for leadership in re-shaping sport for today's men and women, that reflects the requirements of the times and allows for the empowerment of all participants? The answer to this question can best be found when we have a clearer understanding of those social forces that are influencing the vantage points we are taking as we attempt to give meaning to our sports experiences, both as athletes and as spectators.

There are many competing social forces that are inspiration for those articulating a vision about what sports should become. Each of many visions is inspired by a particular configuration of social forces. These voices invite us to follow a variety of different paths. Clearly, each of these voices confidently argues that if we attend to their special message, to the vision they hold, athletes will be empowered by their experiences in sport and hence the world will be a better place. They are reminding us that sport can be empowering when the athlete's competency is affirmed; when sport provides athletes with a sense of belonging; when athletes have earned, through their efforts, their fair share of rewards; when they experience joy and a sense of oneness in the flow of the sports activity itself; when they feel healthy and fit; when they feel they have grown through the experience; when sport provides them with a context in which to develop intimate personal relationships; and when sport has helped them develop the capacity for displaying understanding and concern for those different from themselves.

Further complicating decisions about what direction sport should take is the reality that the sports enterprise has many clients, beside the athletes themselves, whose special interests have to be addressed if sports are to serve the athletes and the community. There are many different investors in the sports enterprise: parents, educational institutions, spectators, the community (the city, state, and nation), sponsors, and professional sports organizations, as well as coaches, officials, sports medicine specialists, and sports event managers. It would be naive, indeed, to think that sports policies and practices can be refashioned in a vacuum, where only the immediate interests of athletes are taken into account. There are many forces that maintain the status quo. And some would argue that sport cannot lead a movement to transform a society that is struggling with changing sex role expectations and other issues of social justice.

Can sport do any more than reflect dominant social values? If society is not ready to accept women as equal partners in making significant political and economic decisions, how can sport be expected to do any more than reflect these social realities? While it is probably true that sport cannot be expected to lead the way to the Good Society, specific sports programs can indeed set out to serve as exemplars of what sport might become. New sports policies and practices need to be fashioned and tested so that men and women are provided opportunities to develop both their masculine and feminine sides through their sports experiences.

In any analysis of sport in society it is important to focus attention on how social and cultural tensions are being played out in the sports context. I have selected the arena of women's sports as a primary focus because I want to share with readers, especially male readers, my reactions to the "culture shock" I have experienced over the past 20 years on my "field trip" into women's sports, shocks that have led me to the values and views I am currently forming. I was allowed by my experiences with my wife and daughters to assume a new vantage point and to zoom in on a new set of features on the "sportscape."

In a sense this is the confession of a convert, not to a pro-female agenda, for I had already committed to that, but to a reframed view of the role of sport in American culture. Even though I had been studying women's issues for 15 years prior to my introduction to women's sports in the mid-'70s, I personally had been so immersed in the mainstream culture of sport that I was insensitive to what was going on around me. To this day, with regularity, I come to insights that cause me to observe with astonishment and embarrassment that I had failed to see an obvious feature of the sportscape earlier on my visit to this seemingly familiar, but often alien, culture. I sometimes feel like a tourist who discovers that he has committed a faux pas as a result of not clearly understanding native mores. It amazes me that, even though I have kept careful "field notes" (and maintained my own album of snapshots) over the past 20 years, I continue to discover so much that is new. My immersion in the institution of gender for over six decades pervades nearly every aspect of my life and has blinded me to many of life's injustices. Just as it is in any cross-cultural study, the visitors are never able to completely get within the frame of reference of the natives in the culture they are studying, even when the natives lend them their special lenses. This limitation has not kept me from refusing to be a man as my awareness has been raised about my restricted "gender vision."

My observations about women's sports are based upon notes I have taken as I have been a participant-observer in the remarkable growth of sports opportunities for women. By paying careful attention I hope I have been able to at least discover the tools that will allow me to better understand the meaning of sport for both men and women. I am greatly indebted to those women who have allowed me to "borrow" their lenses to gain a brighter and fresher perspective on the sportscape.

There are serious limitations to learning how to view the world from the other side. Men in our society, even those who have been taught the scientific tools of socio-cultural analysis, are so thoroughly socialized into the male sports culture that they find it extremely difficult to liberate themselves from limitations of the mainstream perspective on sport. Since "sport talk" is one of the few languages that allow us to communicate with our fellow men, it is difficult to give up the habit. As we know, the lenses we use to view the world and the language we use to describe what we see profoundly influence the ways we perceive and behave. Some of us still have an accent that betrays our roots in a masculine culture that values dominance above all else. This is evident when we use such innocent expressions as "The Oilers really killed them last Sunday." I have come to believe that I am a recovering Jock. My propensity to use military jargon may reflect a malaise from which I am never completely cured, and that I and others must come forward from time to time to acknowledge "My name is David. I am a Jock. I will always be a Jock. Only by the grace of God have I been given relief from the blindness that this condition produces."

As I reflect upon the features of my life that gave rise to my identity as a male, there are hopeful signs that suggest the possibility of recovery. I had a very androgynous upbringing. My mother, a former music teacher, insisted that I learn the fine arts of music, theater, and dance and discouraged me from playing violent sports. As a matter of fact I'm convinced she would have been happy if I had not played sports at all. In school, in addition to being on the basketball and track teams, I played in the band, was a cheerleader, the PA announcer for the football games, a member of the chess team, an actor in school plays, a public speaking contest winner, and active in student government. My father and mother made sure that we as a family had season tickets to the classical concerts, Broadway musicals, and ballet productions that came to our community. I did not miss one Fred Astair or Gene Kelly movie at the old State Theater on Main Street either. Astair and Kelly were the athletes I was taught to admire. And I was the only boy in the community to be afforded that privilege, and for sure I was the only local Jock educated in that manner. What a wonderful gift my parents bestowed upon me! These privileges, not only allowed me to broaden my interests, but also permitted me to develop an aesthetic appreciation of athletic performance.

In addition, I established a significant part of my identity as the "steady" partner of my wife-to-be who I started dating when we were barely 15. Also, I was the son of a community leader and businessman who everyone expected me to succeed. I was not simply Dave

Epperson, jock, but Dave Epperson successor to prominent community leader Sid Epperson.

My father, while beginning his entrepreneurial career as a trucker, which is, without a doubt, one of the more masculine occupations, was also drawn to music and dance and provided a role model that demonstrated that a real man, (he was a commanding six foot three who carried 230 pounds on a large raw boned frame) could also be attracted to the more genteel forms of cultural expression, even though he himself had been an athlete. All those factors conspired to subordinate my identity as an athlete.

Even though I had a successful athletic career and have been involved with sports all of my life, there have always been aspects of my experiences with sports with which I have been uncomfortable. In a sense, I have been an alien in the world of sport from my childhood days (I never collected trading cards or kept baseball statistics), for my identity was never centrally tied to my role as an athlete, even though I spent hours and hours in the gym and on the playing field. As a matter of fact, I can't remember ever having a conversation with one of my boyhood friends when I didn't have a ball in my hand tossing it across the yard or across the room, much to our mothers' dismay.

My lack of involvement with the Trading Card Culture stands in sharp contrast to the experiences of some of my most intimate friends and colleagues, even today. Their identities, decades after their school, college and professional athletic careers, are organized around their experiences with sports. They feel closely connected with the Trading Card Culture, speak the language, and most importantly use that cultural framework to organize their perceptions of the world. Very few of them have had reason to discover new lenses through which to reframe their perspective of the playing field. They genuinely believe they have learned lessons through sports that have allowed them to achieve success in later life, and they reference these learnings just as Secretary Jack Kemp did in an article in *USA Today* "Playing football taught me that nothing happens without inspiration and perspiration...Sports taught me other lessons as well; loyalty, determination, audacity."[4] For those with a core athletic identity I'm sure that not a day goes by that they do not make reference to their experiences with sport, for they can always find someone with whom to test their knowledge, long after they have retired from active competition. As a matter of fact, some of my contemporaries, entering their seventh decade are still active athletes, even after having angioplasty and open heart surgery! While the sports metaphor and my experiences with sport inform my thinking from time to time, it has not been a central definer of who I am, either yesterday or today.

Maybe my commentary on sport cannot simply be understood as the confessions of a recovering Jock, but instead can be better understood as the "coming out" of a closet athlete who denied his feminine side until he found refuge in the comfortable surroundings of women in sports. This not-so-latent side of me may have been struggling to find expression and finally discovered its medium, the world of women's sports administration where traditional masculine and feminine values converge. An interpretation might be that at this point in my life cycle, with my credentials as a Jock in order and being secure in my masculinity, it is now safe to risk giving dramatic, public expression to my feminine side, a side of myself that psychologist Carl Gustav Jung understood that all men possess, but have difficulty expressing.

What is it, then, that can be learned about sport from listening to our feminine voice? The answer seems clear. We can learn to enjoy more fully the processes of sport and give less emphasis to outcomes, and to enjoy the relationships we develop through our lives in sport. We can learn to appreciate the aesthetic and ceremonial aspects of sport that give it not only personal but also socio-cultural meaning. By giving free expression to that feminine voice, we will be in a better position to fashion an approach to sport that enlivens the lives of men and women alike.

In the past, I have labored under the illusion that women could and should chart their own course in sports without worrying about whether men come along. At least for the moment men and their female surrogates hold critical decision-making roles and give little evidence of being the least bit interested in giving up control. Men and women need to understand one another if meaningful change is to occur. Women need a context in which to advance an antithesis to mainstream male-led sports, an initiative that will require a response from the men's side that can eventually lead to a synthesis.

It is my goal to advance an alternative, or an antithesis, if you will, to mainstream sports that appeals to both men and women. When a well-thought out and clearly articulated challenge is issued, a challenge that is firmly grounded in present day socio-cultural realities, then we can expect that both men and women can be mobilized in serious efforts to reframe the sports experience and reform sports policies and practices. This challenge then must be followed by a synthesis of the masculine and feminine perspectives which will become mainstream sports for the New Generation. I want to be a contributor to the creation of a common ground upon which a new approach to sport can be built.

Institutional transformation does not occur with a big bang. Even something as dramatic as the adoption of Title IX, that requires that women be given equal access to quality sports experiences, has resulted in a series of small steps rather than one giant step. Instead, significant change requires a well-orchestrated series of on-going policy adjustments that redirect energy and slowly change what is valued and rewarded. It is for that reason that each and every person, male and female, who has a vested interest in sport, must take the time to inform himself or herself about what steps can be taken to reform sport to meet the requirements of the times.

Cultural Confusion

CHAPTER TWO

Sport, Politics, and
the Greening of America

*There is a revolution coming. It will not be like revolutions of
the past...This is the revolution of the new generation.*

Charles A. Reich
1970

In 1970 in *The Greening of America*[1] Charles
Reich celebrated the dawning of a new level of consciousness. The
emergence of this new perspective was revealed in the highly public
challenges to established values by a new generation of young people
on our college campuses all across the nation. The new generation of
the '60s has become today's old generation. With family responsibilities and grey hair has come a much tamer life style and more conservative politics. While the "baby boomers" have tempered their life
styles and politics, many of the caring and aesthetic values they developed in their youth continue to impact their attitudes and conduct.
Nowhere was this continuity of perspective more evident than in the
1994 PBS documentary, "Hillary's Class." As the story of Hillary
Rodham Clinton's Wellsley class unfolded, it was evident that each
successive generation has had its own unique burdens to bear. Today's
New Generation, the children of the 1969 Wellsley grads, while ben-
efiting from the courage exhibited by their mothers, many of whom
broke with long-standing traditions, face a new set of challenges in the
evolution of women's roles. It is the challenges of the children of the
"graduates" of the cultural revolution of the '60s that have commanded my interest and have provoked my quest for a better understanding
of the role of sport in the gender re-assessment movement.

During this compelling documentary about First Lady Hillary
Clinton's classmates I felt privileged to be able to witness the struggles
of this generation of women, and to try to make sense out of what I had
witnessed. The special vantage point of this work of art allowed me to
come to a better understanding of the challenges that today's men and
women face as they work toward achieving a gender-just world.

Hillary Clinton has become more than simply another First Lady. She has come to represent the hopes and fears of many American men and women. It is evident that not only her classmates but nearly all women admire her for her courage, intelligence, and caring attitude. Some women have difficulty identifying with her specific acts of courage, her style of expressing her intelligence, specific political positions she has taken, or personal economic decisions she has made, but nearly all women can identify with her caring attitude. That is because women in America have all been inducted into a common Culture of Care. What distinguishes Hillary Clinton's generation is that it has participated in public challenges to a social order that has not always allowed for the full expression of their caring predispositions. The protests of the '60s were protests against those forces standing in the way of the full expression of human possibilities. At that point in history the baby boomers, both men and women, were challenging the values of the Culture of Conquest that they identified with waging a distant war; exploiting "Mother Earth"; creating powerlessness among the disenfranchised, the poor, minorities, and women; inventing a culture that encouraged "phoniness"; failing to establish a sense of community; and insisting upon conformity that robs men and women of their individuality. Those who really "care" oppose violence and war, destruction of the environment, oppression of minorities and the poor, the objectification of workers, loss of human connectedness, and actions that produce self estrangement. These are outcomes that have been associated with male-administered policies and practices, that is, with the Culture of Conquest.

Women of that era sensed that all was not well. Sam Keen in *Fire in the Belly* points out that "To the degree that a culture is a warfare system, it will reduce women to second class citizens whose function is essentially to service the warriors."[2] Hillary Clinton and her Wellsley sisters understood what was happening and many followed their lead and challenged the leaders of their era who were wedded to Culture of Conquest solutions to the problems of the times. Hillary's classmates gave her an enthusiastic standing ovation when she departed from her prepared graduation speech to answer the preceding speaker, Senator Edwin Brooks. She took exception to his criticism of the student protest movement. The image of Hillary Rodham challenging a powerful and highly respected leader of a male-led government that was waging a war against both man and nature lingers in the consciousness of her Wellsley classmates.

Each generation creates images that become signs of the times. For the baby boomers the powerful images created by the student protests of the '60s symbolized the tension between that generation of young people and a system they felt had lost touch with basic caring values. The "establishment" was seen as depersonalizing a generation and sending them off to fight a war they did not understand. Who can forget the powerful image of the young woman kneeling over her fallen comrade at Kent State University?

Now that it is the baby boomers' turn to assume control of our social institutions, another set a images has appeared that signals the ascendancy of a quite different set of values on the American scene. These are not images of flower children inserting flowers in the barrels of military rifles, but instead of our national leaders expressing through their conduct values that were rooted in the protests of their youth. The 1993 inauguration of President Clinton signaled that America was entering a new era where the tender values of the student protest movement were finding expression in the new establishment.

The Clinton inauguration left a lasting impression on many of us. Presidential inaugurations are orchestrated so as to provide all citizens with a sense of hope, regardless of their politics. Inaugurations mark a new beginning where the nation reaffirms its commitment to common values and dedicates itself to overcoming what are considered the most difficult problems of the times. Even the cynics find it difficult to keep from harboring at least some shred of hope as they witness the changing of the guard.

On that January day in 1993 our eyes were bathed with unforgettable images: tears streaming down the President-Elect's cheeks as he witnessed "foot stomping" gospel music in an African church; songs performed by an operatic diva and a poem of celebration read by an African-American poet; the new president hugging his vice president at the conclusion of his swearing in; the women in his life preceding the president as he entered the reviewing stand to "Hail to the Chief" for the post-inaugural parade; the new president "jammin" on his saxophone with African-American and white musicians at nationally televised inaugural balls; a president with a wife at his side who has a professional life of her own, and most importantly a mind of her own. These were, indeed, sights to behold, whatever your political persuasion or your assessment of his potential to lead. Nowhere in recent history has it been more evident that we were entering a new era than at the Clinton-Gore inauguration. The "New Age" president, as *Newsweek* described him, represents in his style and values that which George Bush began to articulate with his "kinder and gentler" public rhetoric.

The retiring political and corporate leaders, who were rooted in the military and trade wars of past decades, borrowed the military command and control model to guide the ways they organized for action. Many of today's leaders, including the president, entered adulthood challenging "military-industrial" values.

The requirements for success in this new chapter in the history of America are changing. Many of the baby boomers we have chosen to lead the nation seem to share a commitment to reforming our social institutions in ways that place them more in sync with the values articulated during the '60s protest movement. During the inauguration numerous signs pointed to the fact that we are now beginning to be guided by a new voice. Even though the voice has often been hoarse from engaging colleagues and constituents in lively dialogue, it has had a distinctive gentle, but confident, quality about it that reflects the values and style of a new generation of Americans. Since I am of the so-called "silent generation" that has witnessed the legacy of Hoover and the leadership styles of FDR, Truman, Eisenhower, Johnson, Nixon, Ford, Carter, Reagan, Bush, and now Clinton, I feel especially attuned to the changes in the texture of the voice I am hearing.

President Clinton is at the center of the tension between two major cultural forces that are competing for the minds and hearts of men and women. The images surrounding his inauguration reflected a prominent presence of those qualities emanating from what I am calling the Culture of Care. This set of beliefs and customs competes with the beliefs and customs of the Culture of Conquest. The traditional masculine mores of the Culture of Conquest currently guide the conduct of most American males, but there is increasing evidence that men have begun questioning many of the beliefs of this traditional culture and are finding tender values more in sync with the requirements of the times.

At Clinton's inauguration there were both prominent and subtle signs that indicated that this New Age leadership was repudiating many traditional values and was committed to emphasizing values that support 1) a more tender-minded, feminine, approach to solving the problems of our day, 2) changing sex role expectations where women are able to assume a more prominent role in all aspects of American life, 3) a greater interest in the processes as well as in the outcomes of governance, 4) a more inclusive style of arriving at policies, 5) a clearer understanding of the role of the family in contemporary life, with all of its different forms and complexities, 6) a louder call, especially from Vice President Al Gore for the preservation of "Mother Earth," 7) a stronger commitment to expressing concern for all of the people in this country and throughout the world, and 8) an abhorrence for the violence on the streets that is given impetus by the proliferation of hand guns and automatic weapons.

In short, there are forces at work that are pushing for traditional feminine rather than masculine solutions to today's problems. We are witnessing, what could become that which Charles Reich proclaimed nearly 25 years ago, the "Greening of America." He was celebrating signs of the onset of a new social order where people are being empowered, communities are being enlivened, and both men and women are adopting a new consciousness that puts them on an equal footing. He observed the development of a new outlook that rejected the major themes that grew out of our frontier heritage and the "organization society" where workers were treated as impersonal, interchangeable parts. A generation has passed since Reich offered his interpretation in his best selling book, *The Greening of America*, but the cultural revolution continues. The world has indeed changed. More and more people today are being given opportunities to discover a fuller range of possibilities than in the '60s. A "greening" of most of our institutions, including sport, is well underway.

However, the expression of these "counter cultural" values is occurring in a somewhat different form than Reich predicted. We are beginning to observe a synthesis between the Culture of Conquest and the Culture of Care rather than the replacement of the old with the new. The world can never be as simple or as ideal as Reich conceived of it. A life modeled after the free and uninhibited child is neither consistent with what we know about human nature nor does it have much appeal to those who understand that a richness of life is created by the tension between competing forces in the human situation. Rollo May made an observation in his 1972 book *Power and Innocence* about Reich's vision of the emergent consciousness (Consciousness III):

Far from Consciousness III being an answer, it would be no consciousness at all, for it lacks the dialetic movement between "yes" and "no," good and evil, which gives birth to consciousness of any sort.[3]

While Reich's new level of consciousness has not become the predominant way of viewing the world as he had hoped, there is a residual of the tension created between the Culture of Conquest and the Culture of Care that revealed itself in the youth culture as the boomer generation was growing up. As the results of the 1994 off-year elections and the 1996 congressional elections indicated, President Clinton appears to have been caught in the crossfire between these two cultural forces. Today we can't seem to decide how to reconcile these competing sets of values. The 1994 election results reflect the ambivalence Americans have about the "mandate" they gave Clinton when they sent him to the White House in 1992. The 1994 and 1996 voters seemed to have been calling for lower taxes, smaller government, more personal freedom, hard-line approaches to crime and welfare reform, limited revision of the health-care system, and a return to traditional morals and values. All of these demands can be understood as a backlash to Culture of Care policies that Clinton aspired to put into place. World War II veteran, Bob Dole, battle-hardened former professional quarterback, Jack Kemp, and the intense conservative warrior, Newt Gingrich, were leading the charge.

The emergence of Gingrich as the spokesperson for the congressional opposition to President Clinton underscored the tension between Culture of Conquest and the Culture of Care values and style. While Clinton presents a warm and caring persona, Newt Gingrich displays the studied style of a front-line general. Newt Gengrich reveals a passionate commitment to a military perspective on life. Good people must dominate or be dominated. He is quoted as saying that *The Sands of Iwo Jima* was probably the most formative single film of his life, and that a favorite painting is that of George Washington at the Battle of Princeton. He learned to respect authority and military ideals from his stepfather, a career officer. He proudly worships the "rational," and not surprisingly believes that technology has shaped history and can serve as an answer to many of today's problems. He is said to have a deep feel for human history, but not always for human beings. He is seen as a user in a town of users. He had been selected by his peers to lead the "charge" on the White House, even after being discredited by violations of campaign financing laws. But even the old warrior, Newt Gingrich, has not been completely immune from the "greening" effects of the '60s consciousness raising. He has won the support of the League of Conservation Voters for his stand on air and water pollution. Without question, however, he is a symbol of the backlash to liberal counter cultural values.

I am convinced that Newt Gingrich is not simply a throwback to old-fashioned conservatism. Instead he has become a lightning rod for the expression of frustration Americans are feeling with a government that speaks softly, reveals uncertainty, seems subject to temptations, and appears to accomplish little. He also articulates that side of the American character that distrusts soft, tender, do-gooders, and celebrates the John Wayne-take-charge kind of guy. It should not be surprising that Gingrich reported that he found much of his own story in *Men Who Hate Women & The Women Who Love Them.* Susan Forward's book reported that men who hate women both need and resent the presence of dominating women. And it seemed consistent with his character when his mother reported that he referred to Hillary Clinton as a "bitch." That term is frequently used by men when they are threatened by aggressive women in the workplace. Many American men can identify with his assessment of those women who refuse to be relegated to traditional passive-dependent roles.

Men are not the only ones who use that term to describe "uppity" women. Twelve years ago Barbara Bush referred to Geraldine Ferraro as "a word that rhymes with rich." As women venture into areas previously occupied primarily by men, one can expect both men and women, rooted in the values of the past, to greet such changes with frustration and anger. Labels calm the demons as they rear their ugly heads. Public figures become the voices of our dis-ease.

The tension between the Newt Gengrich and Bill Clinton images is reflected in the tug of war between the Warrior and the Angel that resides deep within the psyches of many Americans, whether they are of the old or the new generation. As we approach the 21st century we are not sure what we want in a leader, because we are uncertain about who we want to be. How the New Generation finally embraces the "Newt Right" has yet to be determined, but there are indications that the leadership of the Republican party demanded that Gingrich maintain a low profile prior to the 1996 convention and campaign when it became evident that the public was put off by his message and style. This public response suggests that the military model is increasingly found to be out of phase with what is required of our social institutions, including sport.

The emergence of Colin Powell on the American political scene has underscored the tension between caring and warring values. The ever popular Powell is indeed a tested warrior, having demonstrated through his life and his soldiering the ability to employ the military model with effectiveness. However, in him we see the emergence of a new military persona, one that reveals a sensitivity to human suffering that tempers his drive to win. He still reflects a commitment to winning as does any good soldier. When asked in an interview with *Newsweek* about his commitment to politics he articulated his attitude toward winning in politics, if he should chose to become a candidate for president. "You don't do it to fool around, you do it to win. And I think that's a pretty good rule for life as well as for military operations."

In his autobiography, *My American Journey*, published in September 1995, Powell observes "I find civility is being driven from our political discourse. . . . We have to stop screeching at each other, stop hurting each other, and instead start caring for, sacrificing for and sharing with each other."[4] He concludes that he is "a fiscal conservative with a social conscience." While he is not a member of the Clinton-Gingrich generation, having come of age in the '50s, unlike many other members of his generation, his caring impulses nevertheless serve to monitor his warrior self. The American public seems to like moderation in a public figure, especially at this point in history. The synthesis Powell displays makes sense, given the realities of our day. His decision not to run for president invited a public skirmish between the tough warrior values of Gingrich, Dole, and Kemp, and the more tender boomer generation values of Clinton-Gore. The fact that we continue to admire successful warriors, whether they achieve success in the military, in politics, in government, or on the playing field reveals that we still want to associate ourselves with winners. But that special breed of winners who temper their winning ways with well-articulated Culture of Care values seem to provide us with the greatest comfort. That is why so many expressed deep regret when Colin Powell dropped out of the presidential race. They saw in him a synthesis between the tough and the tender.

Sam Keen has pointed out:

Even in politics, admiration for the old powermongers, strong men, and iron-willed dictators is being replaced by adulation for a new kind of leader who seeks to empower other—Mikhail Gorbachev, Lech Walesa, Nelson Mandela, and Vaclav Havel.[5]

However, confusion in our public and private realms still reigns and will probably continue to reign for some time to come because Americans are unclear about the role they want government to play in performing care-giving and care-taking functions. Caring values, the desire to empower others, are found in the hearts of nearly all men and women in American. That is our common ground. Who should be providing the care, who should be empowered, and who should be paying for "doing good" are the points of debate. Whether a Democratic president and a Republican Congress can forge a synthesis, only time will tell. Whether a Colin Powell type personality can emerge to help us find a common ground still remains to be determined. The hope lies in the American suspicion of ideology and propensity for pragmatic solutions. Clinton, Gore, Gingrich, Dole, Kemp, and Powell all share a distrust of ideology and have a penchant for the pragmatic. We want our leaders to be visionaries and political operatives who can get things done, not ideologues. Today's political leadership seems to understand that.

While the baby boomers have been consumed by ushering in a cultural renaissance, clearly they have not completely bought into the counter cultural values that prevailed as they were growing up and protesting America's interventions abroad. As they have matured they have become more grounded in economic and political realities and have abandoned many of their romantic and mystical notions about the individual and the community. Communalism and anarchy have given way to communitarianism, and mysticism to worldly-based searches for finding oneself through one's work and family.

There are, however, many prominent observers of cultural change that forsee dire consequences of the legacy of the protest movement of the '60s. Judge Robert Bork, in his book *Slouching Towards Gororrah*, expresses grave concerns about the excesses of

21

egalitarianism and individualism that were promulgated by the counter culture of the '60s. He sees these excesses reflected in policies being advanced by today's liberal political and cultural leaders. He asserts that unless these trends are reversed our culture is headed for disaster. Bork's concluding observation is:

Though I did not expect it then, the charred law books on the sidewalk in New Haven (during the '60s protests) were a metaphor, a symbol of the coming torching of America's intellectual and moral capital by the barbarians of modern liberalism. We have allowed capital to be severely damaged, but perhaps not beyond repair. As we approach its desolate and sordid precints, the pessimism of the intellect tells us that Gomorrah is our probable destination. What is left to us is a determination not to accept that fate and the courage to resist it—the optimism of the will.[6]

The direction of the change is alarming to many conservative observers of American culture, since everywhere they turn they see evidence of compromises of values they hold dear. It seems to them that all of our institutions are not only changing, but that the nature of the change is destroying that which has made our civilization great.

Nowhere are changes in American culture more evident than in the institution of marriage. Today we are moving away from a division of labor, and hence differences in interests, toward a sharing of tasks. That produces more common interests. Even love takes on a new meaning in today's marriages. Warren Farrell, in *The Myth of Male Power*, makes a distinction between marriages of the previous era (Stage I) and those of the present era (Stage II). He understands that as economic, political, and social requirements change, our institutions adapt to these changes.

In Stage I, a woman called it "love" if she found a man who was a good provider and protector; he called it "love" if she was beautiful and could take care of a home and children. Love meant a division of labor which led to a division of female and male interests. In Stage II, love meant common interests and common values. Love's definition is in transition.[7]

The expectations that men and women have for one another are also in transition.

Couples now expect communication skills, joint parenting, shared housework, sexual fulfillment, joint decision-making, a spiritual connection, mutual attraction, and mutual respect. They want both stability and change; both interdependence and a partner who is independent. They want time to grow and time to discover each other's growth. In Stage I, these pursuits would have taken time away from raising children, raising the crops, and raising the money. "Discovering each other" was Stage I's Trivial Pursuit. It threatened survival.[8]

As men and women assume new roles, both outside and inside the home, they find it essential to view the world differently and to expect different things from their institutions: marriage, family, work, religion, and sport. As their roles in the economy change, their attitudes and interests change. Of course, there is not a clear point in time when a person moves from Stage I to Stage II thinking. Today's men and women are working to integrate the best of the cultural traditions they have inherited. Because they are caught between old and new ways of thinking they often seem to be confused and hypocritical in the ways they respond to the requirements of the day and to their representatives in government.

I see New Generation men and women fashioning what I am referring to as a Culture of Counterpoint where the tender, feminine values of the new generation can be integrated with the tough masculine values of both the American Frontier and Industrial Revolution, to create a new texture to American life. It is a culture that allows the masculine and feminine voices within each person to be harmonized. A climate of civility is a prerequisite to the successful blending of masculine and feminine values. Counterpoint describes the process of integrating masculine and feminine traditions. Civility allows for a respectful dialogue that can result in a systhesis that will value questing with care. I use the term questing to refer to the pursuit of a mission. The knights of old went on quests to secure or achieve something for their kingdom. The questors of today are on a mission to achieve the rewards society has to offer, acceptance, fame, and money. Questing is used in contrast to linking which refers to strengthening the fabric of our partnerships, workgroups, families, and communities.

Questing without care both internationally and domestically is what concerned the young people on American campuses in the '60s. "Care-less" questing is what concerns many of today's commentators on contemporary life, including those women activist who are not only striving for equality of opportunity, but who are seeking to position traditional feminine, nurturing values in a more prominent role in the collective lives of men and women.

To many the outcomes of a synthesis of caring and questing are bound to seem confusing and inconsistent, for there are so many distinct voices that have to be blended. These voices are revealed in both the conversations we have with ourselves and with one another. While contemporary men and women still hear the now modulated voices of the '60s protestors, they also are listening to the voices of Gingrich and Bork. The result is often confusion. At the same time I see New Generation men and women making a deliberate effort to integrate the best of both traditions. Extremism always lurks as a possibility, but a blending of the old and the new are most often the outcome when civility prevails.

Counterpoint is a complicated human form, but when it is created with passion and care its effects can be glorious. A climate of civility is a prerequisite for a creative systhesis of the masculine and feminine in human affairs. But we need to make this systhesis happen by providing a legitimate forum in all of our institutions, including sport, so that all voices can be heard. Civility is a prerequisite for knitting together the diverse threads that constitute the fabric of American life. Therefore, the creation of a culture of civility has got to become a high priority item on today's policy making agendas.

No one who has witnessed the gridlock in Washington since the 1993 Clinton inauguration could conclude that the president and the newly elected Congress can easily put into place policies that result in what his predecessor referred to as "a kinder and gentler world." A new conservative Congress, that, in the main, is more comfortable with questing values, will undoubtedly resist adopting social policies rooted in liberal caring values. And the scandals surrounding Clinton's personal conduct have diminished the president's ability to implement the agenda that the elections mandated.

Nevertheless, today's conservatives are no strangers to the Culture of Care, for they too are being influenced in everything they do by the social and economic forces that are keeping the New Generation consciousness alive. They cannot avoid the "greening effects" that have been sweeping America for the past 30 years. We may swerve to the right or to the left, and that may consume precious time, but there is no turning back.

One could conclude that the "wimp" image that haunted President Bush before he went to war with Iraq was a reaction to a pattern of behavior that reflected the dawning of a new era. I am convinced that part of Bush's appeal may very well have been a persona that revealed his feminine side. He was sometimes seen by those immersed in the Culture of Conquest as being too weak, unprepared to "stand up and fight." All this suggests that many Americans seem to be ambivalent about the tender vision that some political leaders are reflecting today, and this uncertainty is making it difficult for the politicians to decide how to play their cards. One thing seems clear. The tension between these two perspectives will not go away, for the economic and political requirements of contemporary life will sustain the chaos. All of our social institutions, including sport, will continue to be battlegrounds where these cultural perspectives struggle for ascendancy. The momentum, however is beginning to lean in the direction of the Culture of Care. As long as women continue to increase their participation in policy formation one can expect movement toward a less harsh and violent world.

There were signs of the times in a handwritten letter from President Clinton to Michigan basketball player, Chris Webber, after the 1993 NCAA Finals, where Webber in the final minute of play called a time out that the team did not have. As a result, a technical foul was assessed which took Michigan out of the game.

Dear Chris,

I have been thinking of you a lot since I sat glued to the TV during the championship game.

I know that there may be nothing I or anyone can say to ease the pain and disappointment of what happened. Still, for whatever it's worth you and your team were terrific.

And part of playing for high stakes under great pressure is the constant risk of mental error.

I know I have lost two political races and made countless mistakes over the last 20 years. What matters is the intensity, integrity and courage you bring to the effort. You can always regret what occurred but don't let it get you down or take away the satisfaction of what you have accomplished.

You have a great future. Hang in there.

Sincerely,
Bill Clinton

There are a number of values reflected in this letter which appear to be rooted in the Culture of Care: Besides affirming that sport is, indeed, an important human enterprise, Clinton is 1) expressing empathy, 2) showing positive regard for Webber, 3) displaying forgiveness by saying that it is human to err, 4) indicating that the processes of sport, the "intensity, integrity and courage" that one brings to the activity, rather than outcomes, are what really count, 5) stating that it is OK to truly enjoy one's accomplishments, that one does not have to always consider oneself to be "in the process" of becoming, and 6) investing Webber with hope. The letter reflects values and a style of leadership that is consistent with the requirements of present day life. It previews a direction that our social institutions, including sport, are taking.

While the policies and practices that give direction to the sports enterprise often are slow to reflect on-going changes in political and economic institutions, they eventually give evidence of being influenced by pervasive social forces. At the moment mainstream sports are profoundly influenced by the values of the Culture of Conquest, where ranking and questing take precedence over linking. In the Culture of Conquest a person's worth is established by his or her capacity to dominate others, to become "top dog." However, there is emerging an ever growing movement that is demanding that sports be guided by values grounded in present day realities. What remains of the counter cultural revolution is reflected in those voices that are calling for "kinder and gentler" institutional policies and practices. Many critics of sport are advocating reforms that are more consistent with what is happening in the larger society: greater inclusiveness, more tenderness, greater acknowledgment of the interconnectedness of the various aspects of sport, more emphasis upon the athlete's developmental processes, more concern for the welfare of others both on and off the playing field, and a greater understanding of the various types of families that are emerging to support their children as they participate in sports. The critics want the world of sport to reflect the current surge of the "female ethos," that is, those values that prevail in the Culture of Care.

Culture of Care virtues were not invented by the radical protesters of the '60s, nor are they alien notions in the history of western civilization. They have been a shadow force throughout all of human history. The teachings of Jesus, as revealed in the New Testament, elevate feminine virtues from a secondary or supportive to a primary or central position in human affairs. This ethic has been a guiding feature of life in America from earliest Colonial times. Historian Riane Eisler, in *The Chalice and the Blade*, contrasts the feminine virtues reflected in Christ's teachings with the masculine virtues that have long prevailed in western culture.

We must not be violent but instead turn the other cheek; we must do unto others as we would have them do unto us; we must love our neighbors and even our enemies. Instead of the "masculine virtues" of toughness, aggressiveness, and dominance what we must value above all else are mutual responsibility, compassion, gentleness, and love.[9]

In America, from the very beginning, there has been a tension between masculine and feminine virtues. Over the past 30 years sport has become a battleground for these two sets of virtues as women have found their way onto the playing field. This battle reveals itself in the tension between the values of the Culture of Conquest and the Culture of Care. This battle is also being played out within today's men and women, that is, in the inner representation of that conflict where there is tension between the Warrior and the Angel within each person.

This recent chapter in the competition between these two forces reflects tension between two perspectives on human nature—the view that men and women are basically self-serving or "bad" and therefore need to be controlled in competition, with the view that men and women are fundamentally caring or "good," if they are not corrupted by their culture. We are being challenged here by something far more profound than simply establishing ground rules for the conduct of the games we play—we are experiencing the perennial tension that exists between two competing world views that reveal themselves to each person and to each generation in one form or another.

In my judgment, the emergence of women in sport is influencing the way we are now viewing sport. As carriers of the values of the Culture of Care they have been leaving their imprint upon the institution of sport. Even though their activities have taken on much of the flavor of male-led mainstream sports, the identity of most women, including tomboys, is still profoundly affected by their upbringing as women. While they may publicly embrace traditional masculine values, most female athletes are still first and foremost women. The women's sports community, then, holds within itself the potential for initiating reforms in sport that can put this enterprise more in tune with the realities of present day life.

The majority of women's sports leaders has made significant compromises to establish themselves with their male counterparts, who still control the purse strings. Fortunately, there are some courageous women administrators with roots in the old AIAW women's sports federation that governed women's athletics before it was cooped by the NCAA, who persevere in their efforts to preserve the values of the Culture of Care. However, these valiant leaders, in isolation, cannot be expected to assume full responsibility for leading the way toward sports reform. Most of the younger women leaders have yielded to the dominant sports culture in order to gain respectability with those who maintain control over their budgets, that is, male athletics directors. These women's leaders, who some would conclude have "sold out" to Culture of Conquest standards of conduct, along with their male colleagues and mentors, continue to aggressively transmit their values to young women athletes. In the long run their efforts will be in vain. Most young women who have been socialized into Culture of Care values and who are being affected by the forces that are bringing about change throughout all of our social institutions will resist efforts to stamp out their feminine, caring qualities. Without a doubt, there is a backlash as there has always been when "pushy women" have insisted upon having their way, but it appears that this time there are just too many forces supporting the "greening" of our cultural institutions for the trend to be easily reversed.

When Professor Henry Higgins in *My Fair Lady* sings "If only a woman—were more like a man" he is expressing the frustration that men, through the ages, have experienced when they have attempted to transform women into their image. Like Professor Higgins most men are not ready to celebrate *le difference*, neither when they are mentoring nor when they are competing with women. What we are witnessing today in nearly all of our male-led institutions, including sport, is that women are being offered opportunities to enjoy the benefits of participation, if they are willing to adopt a masculine mode of operation. The argument that is made is that the very nature of traditional male tasks requires a tough, masculine approach. Therefore, if women are to perform these tasks they need to employ male means. In spite of significant changes that have taken place in sex role socialization since Victorian times, dramatic differences in the way men and women are taught to approach the world still exist and affect how they chose to enact their respective roles.

Historically, men have been trained to be tough, distant, active, and task-oriented. In other words, they have been trained to serve as warriors so that the interests of their families and communities can be protected. Women, on the other hand, have been educated to be tender, close, passive, dedicated to maintaining harmony in relationships, and salving their warrior's wounds. Men have been expected to use their toughness to do battle "out there" in the cold, cruel, competitive world. Women, on the other hand, have been expected to use their tenderness to care for family members who have returned to the safety and comfort of the warm hearth. The pervasiveness of these sex role differences over time, across class, race and ethnic boundaries, has provided the basis for much contemporary discussion and debate about gender equity, since more and better opportunities are usually available to individuals who demonstrate masculine styles of relating to the world, wherever they might be located in the social structure. Traditionally most high status jobs have been those that are thought to require tough rather than tender qualities. Women who have wished to enter non-traditional careers have had to signal clearly that they were, indeed, physically and mentally tough enough to cope with the inevitable "real world" tests of skill and determination. For example, Senator Diane Feinstein of California, when she ran for mayor of San Francisco, had as her slogan: *Toughness Doesn't Always Come in a Pinstriped Suit*. But American men and women, at this point in time are ambivalent about what to think about achieving women. In the O.J. Simpson criminal case prosecuting attorney, Marsha Clark, submitted to a cosmetic makeover so that she would appear softer and hence be more appealing to the jury, the judge, the press, and the public. Women continually have to prove that they are strong enough to occupy non-traditional roles, but we still expect them to remain soft and "feminine." There remain many who have to be convinced that women are really tough enough to engage in serious athletic competition, in spite of substantial evidence that women can persevere under the most challenging of circumstances.

There are some who have concluded that sport for both men and women would benefit greatly from an infusion of feminine, caring ways. And then there are those who are convinced that sport provides a perfect arena for women to learn the toughness they need to cope with the realities of competition out there in the rough and tumble world of corporate America.

Those responsible for programming sports experiences for the New Generation cannot escape being in the crossfire between the Culture of Conquest and the Culture of Care. Parents, coaches, and educational policy makers, however, cannot wait until the smoke clears from the battlefield to decide on how to reconcile these two competing forces. As they make day to day decisions they need a vision to guide their actions. By coming to a better understanding of the nature of the social forces that are making their decisions difficult they will be able to proceed with intelligence. Hopefully, they will listen closely to their inner voices so that they can hear more clearly the messages coming from their feminine side. When both men and women begin listening to their gentle feminine voices, sport will be able to move from being a male construction to being a human construction. Also when men and women listen carefully to both their masculine and feminine voices, sport will be able to move from being a battleground to being a common ground in the war between the sexes. A climate of civility must prevail before a common ground can be found. Civility requires that men and women stop shouting and accusing and start listening and respecting. When that occurs, a common ground can be established and sport will be better able to perform its primary function of renewing the human spirit.

CHAPTER THREE

Inside the Women's Gym: A Father's Surprising Discovery

It was 1966 on a hot August day in Champaign, Illinois when the doctor came into the waiting room to proclaim, *"IT'S A GIRL."* One of my first reactions was, "Thank God, no Little League!" Not in my wildest dreams did I imagine what was to become our shared destiny, for the farthest thing from my mind was spending long hours encouraging young girls as they tested themselves in the gym and on the playing field. Nor 22 months later when our second daughter was born did we consider the possibilities of following them from coast to coast as they engaged in the quest for athletic excellence. Most assuredly, if our children had been boys, at their birth we would have received gifts of balls, bats, and other athletic gear that would have prepared us for what was to come.

When I first cast my eyes on these precious children with their delicate fingers and fine features, I was impressed by their fragile nature and my instincts were to protect them from all manner of harm. It would not be the last time I would be reminded of the vulnerability of young women as they experience life's passages. Nor was it the last time the instinct to protect them from a potentially hostile world would well up inside me. Our daughters' decisions to pursue athletic excellence routinely put them at risk and frequently provoked our protective instincts.

The journey my wife and I shared with both of our daughters took us often onto the playing field and into the gym. It was there that the entire family learned so much about ourselves, our relationships, about important human values, about the challenges young women face as they attempt to carve out a role for themselves, and about both the beauty and ugliness of sports. Often times we were unprepared for the lessons we were forced to learn. It has been clear to me over the years that we have been joined on our journey by fellow travelers, both parents and sports educators, who have been frustrated by their experiences in the world of sports. They too are searching for ways to make life better for their daughters, or in the case of coaches for those athletes in their charge.

As with all significant investments, sports contain potential risks and benefits. While it is true that only the athletes are on the playing field and are the ones who are at risk and who must possess the courage to compete, those on the sideline are, indeed, "in the game," that is, their skills as parents, siblings, sports educators, and supporters of women's sports are also put to the test. At this point in the history of the development of sports for women challenges have been issued to all concerned.

An adventure into serious sports training is nearly always a significant phase in the lives of sportswomen and their families. This opportunity for mutual discovery passes all too quickly. If one is to take full advantage of the opportunities sports offer, it is necessary to be prepared to grasp the moment. The significance of the sports experience for the dedicated athlete and the fleeting nature of this experience inject a sense of urgency into searching for ways to inspire policy makers and practitioners to take their mission seriously. An act of Congress more than two decades ago helped define the importance of sport for women (Title IX of the Equal Opportunities Act). But much still remains to be done.

Sports have always been an important feature in my life, in the neighborhood learning to become a "man," at school learning to become a vital member of the community, and at college learning to become a contributor to my chosen field, and as an adult sharing athletic moments with my family and friends. I must confess, however, that in my younger days as I was participating in athletics I gave sports little thought except as they added to the enjoyment of my life.

Since sports have always been such a natural feature of "growing up male," they faded into the background and commanded little critical attention for most of us. The only time I was faced with a significant decision about sports was in choosing a career. However, that decision, for me, was relatively simple. I had never really aspired to become a sports educator, although I had accepted coaching assignments in both the military and at the junior high school where I spent my first year of teaching.

It was when our oldest daughter came home from the sixth grade and announced that the boys had selected her to play on the school basketball team that we were caused to pay serious attention to sports. Through the local Y our girls had been provided opportunities to participate in those activities girls traditionally choose, that is, dance, swimming, ice skating, and gymnastics. But it never really occurred to us that they might someday decide to enter into serious athletic training in one of these or in any other sport, for that matter. And for sure, we were not prepared for how their decisions would impact our lives.

As parents we assume responsibility for protecting our children from unnecessary pain and suffering. Those are natural parental instincts. Every time our children enter into a new activity, while we want them to grow and develop in the process of addressing their unique challenges, we do not want them to be exposed to the consequences of failure. Yet, we know that growth can only occur when they develop the courage to venture into uncertain territory. As our daughters began their athletic careers we wanted them to be provided with the support they needed to take those risks. We didn't want them to get into situations where they would be dis-couraged and lose confidence in their ability to succeed. In short, we, like all parents, always want our children to feel OK about themselves, to be empowered and enlivened, so that they can develop the courage to live their lives fully.

There are many features of life in contemporary America that send messages to young women to make them feel that there are some territories where they are less than welcome. In regard to sports, little girls are currently being sent mixed messages. On the one hand, they are being told that they live in a new era where old sex role limitations no longer apply, that girls can become whatever they desire, even an astronaut. Consider engineer, Dr. Tammy Jernigan, the former Stanford volleyball player who traveled into space on 1991,1992, and 1995 NASA missions. On the other hand, there are still many messages that communicate that girls are better served if they choose more traditional paths where they can develop the skills necessary to be nurturing wives and mothers.

These are difficult times for young women. Society is inviting them into highly competitive arenas, yet to accept that invitation exposes them to risks for which many are not yet prepared. That is why it is so important for them to be assisted to develop the confidence and courage to venture into the unknown. Unfortunately, the current support system available as they walk onto the playing field is often less than adequate for giving them the gift of courage.

Those of us who have had reason to observe "up close and personal" our daughters' exposure to risk in the athletic arena have learned several things. First of all, the support system for sportswomen is meager at best and is not getting better quickly enough to protect the current generation of athletes from malpractice, negligence, excesses and abuses. This is abundantly clear when reflecting back upon our family's early experiences with girls sports in the mid-'70s. As our daughters tried out for their junior high and club teams the shortcomings of the women's sports training system became immediately apparent. The problem of achieving equity persists today and in some cases is more desperate as school districts struggle to balance their budgets. In most schools across the nation there have been cutbacks that have resulted in serious limitations on athletic budgets. While it affects boys sports as well, the outcomes are much more damaging for girls, since their sports programs are in a more primitive stage of development. Furthermore, the veteran football, basketball, and baseball coaches are still, in most cases, employees of the schools and are available to serve the boys. Not so on the girls side, for there are few veteran coaches of girls and more often than not they are pressed into service to coach more than one sport. This limits their opportunities to develop high levels of coaching competency in any of their assigned sports. And the majority of coaches available are not regular members of the school's teaching staff. In fact, there are still many school and college coaches of women who are walk-ons and do not participate at all in the general education of athletes.

What is the net result of this move toward economic retrenchment at a time when women's sports are just getting off the ground? Girls are exposed to greater risk of being held back or even damaged by inept coaching. This unintended outcome simply perpetuates inequities found in other sectors of society. That is, indeed, an unfortunate outcome since girls are not generally trained through the normal course of growing up to routinely cope with the frustrations and setbacks that are inevitable in serious sports competition. They have been the children of parents who have understood it is their responsibility to protect their daughters from unnecessary anguish. Therefore, if young girls are to participate enthusiastically in sports they need to be encouraged, otherwise they will begin to doubt their ability to develop into competent human beings. Beyond that, they and their families need to be taught how to re-form the system of resource allocation that has given rise to these limiting cultural expectations and inequities.

It is impossible to separate the issues of sports program quality from general societal issues of gender equity. Without increased appropriations for women's athletics the opportunities for young women to develop the capacity to be empowered by sport will be diminished. Already, far too many experiences dis-courage women as they seek to be taken seriously and find their way to productive roles in society. Sports should not add to the burden of young women as they search for ways to live their lives with strength and courage.

In Jane Wagner's brilliant play, *The Search for Signs of Intelligent Life in the Universe*, Lilly Tomlin's character, Trudy, was chosen by alien visitors to serve as a tour guide of this "planet in puberty." In 1977 when I began my tour of the alien world of women's sports, which at that point was more like a "planet in infancy," I did not have the benefit of tour guides, let alone ones as insightful as Wagner and Tomlin. My adventures and misadventures onto this unfamiliar turf have caused me to seriously re-examine my perspective on sport. I am eternally grateful to my daughters, whose fledgling sports careers launched me on a 20-year trek through a "sportscape" that appeared on the surface to be so familiar but in reality turned out to be difficult to negotiate for a male so thoroughly socialized in the Culture of Conquest in small town America in the '30s and '40s.

It was a rainy wintry day in Northern California when my wife and I drove our daughters to their very first volleyball tournament. At that stage in the development of the sport there were few, if any, junior tournaments, so their dedicated and ambitious junior high and club coach enrolled them in a C level women's event where they could experience competition in the off-season. I really don't know what I expected, but quite honestly I was more than pleasantly surprised by what I discovered on that bleak day in that dark dingy gym. Quite remarkably, and unexpectedly, that day was a major turning point in my life and in the life of our family.

The competitors that day, with the exception of our daughters and their teammates, were mature women who had chosen to continue their sports careers into adulthood. The atmosphere in the gym was magnificent! The athletes were competitive, not contentious. The matches were filled with joy and excitement. Everyone took the games seriously and played their hardest, diving with reckless abandon to the floor to make heroic saves. Yet with all of its seriousness, there was a real up-beat mood that prevailed, whether the teams won or lost. There was no stomping around, contesting referee's calls, ragging on one's teammates, and other modes of conduct that have come to characterize so much of mainstream sports today. What impressed me most was the genuine interest that the competitors showed in one another. That was unprecedented in my experience as an athlete. During my athletic career in school, college, and the military, never once was I encouraged to have more than two words with an opponent, and that was either "good luck" or "good game."

That day, between matches, the women chatted among themselves, thoroughly enjoying, not only competing against one another, but also sharing special off-court moments. The athletes had chosen to make this day-long tournament a true family outing, inviting their husbands, friends, children, moms and dads to share their athletic moments. A real sense of community had been created that brought together three generations. Sport for all of us in that gym, whether we were competitors or spectators, uplifted our spirits, regardless of who won or lost the scheduled matches. Sport provided a common ground upon which to build relationships. Maybe the candidates in the 1992 presidential election were unable to agree upon the meaning of family values, but on that day I experienced a sense of connectedness with my children, the other athletes, and their families that was indeed precious. I believe that everyone, Democrats and Republicans alike, would agree that the values that reigned that day are ones that everyone in America would like to see perpetuated. Those wonderful, but at that time, alien sports experiences propelled me on a 20-year-long mission to support those all too rare signs of intelligent life in sport.

This is not to say that I had never experienced uplifting moments in my own sports career, which at that point had spanned four decades. For I, as a hometown hall of famer, had frequently had my moments of exhilaration in the gym and on the playing field and had experienced the recognition and camaraderie that sport offers. But there was something quite different about the atmosphere in that gym that day that changed forever the meaning of sport for me and my family.

That was the good news. The bad news was to follow. First of all, the more we threw ourselves into supporting our daughters' school and club athletic programs, the more we became aware of the dreadful inadequacies and inequities that exist in the world of sports. While our daughters were frequently coached by classroom teachers with little or no experience with the sport, who had been "volunteered" to assume a coaching assignment, the young men in those same schools had access to coaches with decades of experience as both athletes and coaches. Five out of seven of my daughters' first coaches had either never played or never coached the sport they were assigned! But that's another story. Right now I want to go beyond issues of equity and examine what the sports experience has come to mean to me.

The story I want to tell here is about what has happened to me "on my way to the forum," that is, the girl's gym (if, indeed, I was fortunate enough to find one). During my 20-year excursion into women's sports, I have had an inside view of its evolution. While there is, of course, a long laundry list of deficiencies that need to be remedied, there are unquestionably developments that deserve to be celebrated.

In this chapter I have chosen one critical problem to address and one encouraging segment of the women's sportscape to celebrate. The problem can be simply stated: The more women's sports grow and achieve public credibility and visibility, the more they begin to mimic the excesses and abuses of the Culture of Conquest and the more they lose those precious uplifting qualities that attracted me to the activity in the first place. This is a frustrating paradox. The greater our success in promoting women's sports, the more they are corrupted by the growth-inhibiting practices that have for so long plagued sport in America. I guess it would be unreasonable to expect it to be otherwise. But it is, indeed, a cost of success I am unwilling to accept without challenge.

On the other hand, I see no diminution in those positive, nurturing qualities that women bring to sports. Most women athletes, except for those few who have totally bought into the military model that governs the Culture of Conquest, genuinely want to have intense, vigorous, competitive sports experiences that are empowering, connecting, and enlivening, without the excesses and abuses. Most women in our culture possess within themselves the tendencies to fashion sports environments that include the qualities I experienced at my first volleyball tournament. They are inclined to seek experiences that allow them to celebrate their connectedness to their fellow men and women, intuitively attempting to recover, through sports, the dignity and sense of significance that is frequently denied them in other aspects of their lives. It is through my experiences with women in the gym and on the playing field that I have come to understand that sport does not need to be the bastion of male chauvinism where the avoidance of defeat becomes an obsession, but instead should be understood as a celebration of human possibility and communion that can, when appropriately orchestrated, restore human dignity to all participants, athletes, coaches, parents, and spectators alike. We all need to pay attention to expressions of this feminine predisposition if sport is to serve an enlivening function in the human community.

One possibility that may seem radical to some, and unrealistic to others, is that women take the initiative to lead men to rediscover sport so that it can be restored to performing its essential function of uplifting the human spirit. This would not be the first time in American history that women have helped men "find religion." Sport can have a higher calling and women who have not yet been contaminated by the Culture of Conquest can point the way. Enlightened souls in the women's sports community can indeed provoke "the search for signs of intelligent life" in sport. It may be the case that there are enough men out there who would be greatly relieved to be "rescued" from having to engage in traditional male posturing. They may welcome the opportunity to drop the "testosterone curtain" long enough to be able to connect with their fellow men and women. Maybe it is possible for men and women to join together in search of signs of intelligent life in sport.

What do we mean by signs of intelligent life? What signs would we accept that intelligent life does, in fact, exist? In my view, those signs can be discovered and they are more likely to be found in those women's sports activities that have not been infected with the viruses that emanate from the Culture of Conquest.

It needs to be made clear that I am not criticizing the emphasis upon either competition or the "will to win," for it is essential for athletes, male and female, to be put to the test by their opponents if they and the spectators are to be treated to an enlivening contest. Christopher Lasch in *The Culture of Narcissism* understands clearly what is wrong with the current direction sport has taken:

Sport has come to be dominated not so much by an undue emphasis upon winning as by the desperate urge to avoid defeat. Coaches, not quarterbacks, call the plays, and the managerial apparatus makes every effort to eliminate the risk and uncertainty that contribute so centrally to the ritual and dramatic success of any contest. When sports can no longer be played with appropriate abandon, they lose the capacity to raise the spirits of players and spectators, to transport them into a high realm of existence.[1]

If the Culture of Conquest that currently governs most sport is failing to guide women in a direction that raises the spirits of athletes and spectators and transports them into higher realms of existence, then what alternative should we consider?

Maybe we can take a clue from Lilly Tomlin's Trudy. From her alien visitors she learned the practice of awe-robics. Awe-robics are described as an exercise designed to develop the capacity to experience awe, a term which, if applied to the athletic experience, might lead us to re-examine some of the assumptions we make, the policies we adopt, and the sports practices we support.

There is no question but that quality sports are those where one witnesses awesome performances and actively participates in breathtaking celebrations. Contrary to common wisdom, spectating is not a passive vocation as any observer of a lively NBA or NFL game will attest. Watch parents witnessing their children on the playing field and you will be convinced that spectating is indeed a lively activity! During the 1992 and 1993 NCAA Women's Division I Volleyball Championships I found myself spending as much time watching one of my friends live and die on each play as she cheered on her daughter as I did watching the game itself. Watching one's child compete is without question a lively activity with uplifting possibilities if one has invested in developing the capacity to enjoy the aesthetics of the actions of the athletes. If one focuses exclusively on the outcome, the experience can be frustrating and dispiriting.

When we find ourselves asking "How in the world did the athletes on the playing field accomplish that feat?" we know we have experienced something very special. Awe-robics then are breathtaking (rather than breath giving as are aerobics). Sports are best when we enjoy wonder, amazement, enchantment, and astonishment, when we experience the uneasiness, maybe even the fear, that goes with the uncertainty of what will happen next (Will our team be able to overcome this or that obstacle?) and when we display genuine respect for the participants in rituals of sport: the athletes, the coaches, the spectators, and the supporting cast (referees, cheerleaders, bands, etc.).

Sports are also best when athletes show respect for themselves and their bodies. An awesome sports performance engenders all of those things, wonder, fear, enchantment, and respect.

Maybe awe-robics is not such an alien notion after all. Is it possible we can discover new ways of thinking about sport guided by the goal of creating awesome experiences for all involved? What would happen, if instead of asking the question, "How can we prepare athletes to avoid defeat? we were to ask, "How can we create an awe inspiring, uplifting experience for all concerned?" If we were to ask the latter question it seems apparent that the norms and values of the Culture of Conquest would no longer be appropriate. What kind of a cultural model, then, should we use to guide our actions?

In my search for an alternative to the Culture of Conquest where sport is driven by the need to conquer, I have determined that the new model must encourage participants to be driven by the need to be enlivened or renewed, or if a religious metaphor would be more expressive, to be reborn. Where in our mass culture do we have institutional arrangements where enlivenment and emotional renewal are primary reasons for being?

The answer seems to be that nearly all institutions have the potential for performing these functions of enlivenment and renewal, for they have in place regularized ceremonies designed to raise the spirits of their participants. Whether its a corporate retirement party, a product announcement show, a school graduation, a church service, or a military ritual, these ceremonial events possess the potential of raising the spirits of the participants. It might be useful to view sports performances as ceremonies that serve this renewal function. We are not talking about sports as simply pastimes, but as well-orchestrated rituals designed to achieve individual and collective renewal, where everyone who leaves the "chapel" feels empowered because they have been engaged and invested. That is, everyone has been caught up by the collective energy which was created by ritualized vigorous competition that demanded an emotional investment by all concerned.

The players not only compete; they enact a familiar ceremony that reaffirms common values. Ceremony requires witnesses: enthusiastic spectators conversant with the rules of the performance and its underlying meaning.

Can raising human spirits through the enactment of a familiar ceremony become a primary justification for sport? I think so. Sport's fundamental "reasons for being" could very well be to empower participants and enliven communities. If athletes learn skills and values that serve them well as they move through life, so much the better. But if a sports experience can do no more than give participants the courage to stand tall, then it will have achieved an invaluable objective, an outcome that would be enthusiastically welcomed as we enter this new era.

Where else can we gain access to this type of renewal of the human spirit. In a secular society where sport has become one of the few activities that serve to connect individuals from all sectors through shared involvement in local, regional, and national competitions, it offers a ready-made context in which both men and women can find a common ground for communal celebration. Sport can cut across religious, racial, and economic barriers and allow for collective appreciation of human performance and give participants a glimpse of human possibility.

Before each Stanford Basketball game my teammates and I gathered in a huddle to join in the following incantation:

> *One for all*
> *All for one*
> *All for Stanford University*

Then we would charge onto the court with the band playing the "Stanford Fight Song" and the cheerleaders leading the crowd in an exuberant cheer, dramatically punctuating our sacred chant. Those were awesome moments of anticipation, for the coach, the athletes, the referees, and the spectators.

Those were not, however, the only goose bumps we experienced each time we were privileged to put on a Stanford uniform. When the team left the locker room, before even entering the arena, we were filled with excitement, and when we entered the old Encina Gym to the first greeting from the assembled crowd, we were always treated to an experience that took our breath away.

Throughout every game there were many times when the athletes, coaches, referees, and spectators were able to jointly participate in those special athletic moments. These are the wonderful awe-robic experiences that Lilly Tomlin as Trudy in *The Search for Signs of Intelligent Life* so cogently described.

When she took her alien visitors to the theater she asked them for their reactions. They replied "The play was soup, the audience was art." And before they left for outer space they commented that, "The thing we remember the most about being on this planet was the Goose Bump Experience." The message here is that uplifting responses to life's experiences are often more important than the events that provoke them. It was my emotional reactions to those glorious moments on the Stanford court, the feelings of closeness to my teammates, the sense of rootedness in the traditions of the college community that enlivened my life, not the specifics of the events that provoked the responses. The memories of the reactions remain, while the specifics have become blurred.

Sport may perform other functions as well, but if it is used in the service of goals other than to make participants feel powerful, connected, and uplifted, it is more often than not corrupted. When sport becomes a vehicle for promoting the superiority of one nation over another, as it has become in the Olympic community, its capacity to raise the spirits of the participants, athletes and spectators alike, is often diminished. It is all too apparent that athletes are being used to accomplish another purpose. In these circumstances they become objects to be polished by any means necessary, drugs, psychological abuse, etc., in the service of the state. In a quality sports experience athletes are instead treated as subjects who are major players in celebrations of achievement and community.

The same can be said when sport is used in the service of achieving the fitness of citizens, as reflected in accomplishing the mission of the President's Council on Physical Fitness. Citizens are urged to participate in fitness-producing sports so that our nation will again be strong. "Flabby citizens make for flabby soldiers" who will be less able to protect our national political and economic interests the argument goes. Clearly, there is nothing wrong with the promotion of fitness. However, when athletes are used to accomplish national health maintenance goals the ceremony of sport can lose its ability to produce uplifting astonishment.

Likewise, when sport becomes a means to social reform or character building the activity, more often than not, loses its capacity for achieving its awe-inspiring mission. As attractive as it might seem, using sport as a way of teaching athletes skills and attitudes for effective competition, that are commonly (and most likely erroneously) believed to be essential for success in the "real world" has the same effect. Such uses of sport often deaden rather than enliven the human spirit. The key here is that athletes are being used for political, social, or economic ends, not as citizens who have assumed a special role to help orchestrate human communion.

Agreeing to participate as a major player in a community ceremony (as either paid or unpaid celebrants) is quite different from being used to achieve another purpose, such as to raise funds for a college. As celebrants, athletes are being brought onto a team of participants whose goal is to be uplifting and as a consequence be uplifted by the experience of athletic competition. Contrary to what many commentators allege, paying athletes to perform as celebrants does not necessarily corrupt the spirit of sport. Using sport to accomplish other ends often times does.

If we open our minds and hearts as we accompany our daughters on their adventures into the world of sports we will be able to discover masculine and feminine possibilities within ourselves and in the situations we share with them. Not only will this personal discovery allow us to be more helpful to our children as they make their way along this sometimes rocky pathway to maturity, but we too, as their mentors, can grow and develop into more fully functioning human beings. By elevating our vantage point on sport we will be in a better position to share in our daughters' joy as they are uplifted by quality sports experiences, but we will also be able to experience sports in ways that are enlivening to us as well.

As we and our daughters grow together we will be able to contribute to the creation of those special shared moments when energy flows in both directions, where there is a synergy between parent and child. The more able we are to articulate a fresh perspective on sport, one that reflects both masculine and feminine values, the tough and the tender, the more likely we are to be able to help our daughters enjoy their sports experiences. They will then be empowered, not only by developing the capacity to contribute to their own welfare, but also by being able to contribute to the well being of all those on the sportscape with whom they come into contact, their coach, teammates, parents, spectators, and other investors in the sports enterprise. This allows us to do our part in creating a growth-enhancing balance in the sports ecosystem. We will have contributed to the "Greening of the Playing Field," a renewal mission that desperately needs our loyalty and devotion.

CHAPTER FOUR

Wanted: Pretty Woman with Balls

Zooming in on an incredibly popular Hollywood movie, *Pretty Woman*, may inspire hope for those of us searching for a new lens through which to view the "sportscape." Never mind that a movie with that kind of a title and theme is likely to infuriate those feminists who have devoted their lives to battling both the Beauty Myth and the Cinderella Myth. This screenplay, that chronicles a chance meeting of a prostitute and a charming, but driven corporate mogul, may tell us more about ourselves and the battle between the masculine and feminine forces in our lives than is apparent upon first viewing.

While restlessly flipping the channels, on a number of occasions I have happened upon *Pretty Woman*. Each time, to our amazement, my wife and I have been engaged by whatever scene in the movie we have intercepted and have both chosen to view the movie through to its conclusion. (This is something that occurs from time to time when we happen upon one of the classics, such as *Casablanca*.) Each time we have stayed with *Pretty Woman* we have been puzzled by our fascination with the film and have asked ourselves why we have been so engaged by this simple fantasy. Obviously, we are not alone, since the film continues to draw high viewer ratings. At first we thought it might be that the personalities of the actors, Julia Roberts and Richard Geer, were engaging to us and other enthusiastic viewers. Then we speculated that maybe the Cinderella theme was what was grabbing us. It was not until I was immersed in writing about masculine and feminine forces in sport that I began to understand why we and so many others have been captured by this classic rags-to-riches story.

Greek myths retain their interest over time because they represent perennial human dilemmas that can be found at each stage in the evolution of humankind. I'm not suggesting that *Pretty Woman* is worthy of being considered a classic, but possibly this film is a modern day myth that reflects a recurrent theme couched in the American culture of the '90s. Some would interpret the film as a social mobility fantasy that serves to perpetuate the dream of rescue from limited circumstances. Such an interpretation would position this work of art as a safety valve for a social system that provides little real opportunity for upward mobility. Undoubtedly, for many the story does, indeed, act as a safety valve. It gives many viewers the hope that they too may someday escape from the limitations that bind them. But I have come to understand *Pretty Woman* to be more than an updated Cinderella saga.

The principals in this script are the Richard Geer character, Edward Lewis, a remarkably successful capitalist who buys companies, breaks them up into smaller units and then sells them at handsome profits, and the Julia Roberts character, Vivian Ward, a hooker, who has only recently taken up her profession. Having just come off of a failed marriage and a lifeless romance Edward is enchanted by this spirited woman who brings into his life a fresh perspective.

From the outset it is made clear that Edward is a driven, task centered, competitive man who is consumed with the desire to gain control over others. It is also made apparent that he has little capacity for caring and intimacy. The motive that drives this success oriented, refined gentleman appears to be the desire to outdo his successful, capitalist father who abandoned him and his mother early in his life. It is also disclosed that he regularly fails when it comes to establishing intimacy with his lovers, his family, and his friends. He is clearly in need of being rescued from this recurrent pattern. He needs to be re-scripted, and Vivian is the designated writer of new dialogue.

On the other hand, Vivian, who has only an 11th grade education, is portrayed as a person who has the capacity for caring for and establishing intimacy with her friends. But she is not educated in the refinements of life. She has much to learn if she is going to escape her street walking life style and realize her potential. She is a bright, high spirited young woman.

The charm and humor of their relationship resides in their radically different backgrounds, or vantage points. It is clear from the beginning where this plot is going. He is going to be rescued, forever transformed by this chance meeting, and she too will be radically changed by allowing herself to experience the world in new ways.

One of the ground rules they establish early in their relationship is that there will be no "kissing on the lips." In other words, they were signaling to one another that they will not allow any real intimacy to enter into their relationship. All viewers realize at the moment they enter into this contract that it will be violated before it is all over and that they are destined to find a common ground. This common ground is found, in part, when they are both emotionally moved by a performance of the San Francisco Opera Company, her first experience with that art form. This experience breaks down the cultural barriers between them and allows them to share a few precious moments. It seems apparent to me that sport, as well as the arts, offers opportunities to share special goose-bump-producing episodes together.

I have come to understand the rescue drama of Edward and Vivian as a reflection of the universal tension between masculine and feminine predisposition, between a task-centered and a person-centered orientation to life, between the tough and the tender. These two characters are playing out the drama that nearly all contemporary men and women experience in one form or another. The universal nature of their dilemma explains at least in part why this film has been such a box office hit. We can all relate to the underlying conflict within ourselves between the tough masculine disposition to achieve and the tender feminine tendency to care that is played out in everyday life. We all have come to feel incomplete to some degree when we are unable to develop the capacity for either achievement or intimacy. At some level we all would like to embody both Edward's drive to succeed and Vivian's caring and intimacy.

We are uplifted in the end when it becomes clear that they are being rescued from their respective limitations. I have chosen to interpret the final scene when Edward overcomes his fear of heights and triumphantly climbs the fire escape to express his commitment to Vivian, with Vivian meeting him half way, as a confirmation that they have both acquired the courage to cross the Golden Bridge (that passageway between the masculine and feminine worlds) and are allowing themselves to savor the fruits of experiencing the other side.

The box office success of this double-rescue, Cinderella fantasy makes me believe that one of the more urgent challenges modern man and woman face as they live their lives together is to figure out ways they can rescue one another from traditional, but limiting, ways of doing things. The playing field is one place where masculine and feminine approaches to life are being dramatically contested. Sport provides a context in which to evaluate the appropriateness of these two quite different approaches to meeting the requirements of contemporary life.

We need to make two kinds of changes if there is to be a synthesis of these traditional outlooks. First of all, we must change our perceptions of what we are observing. We need to re-frame sports experiences, using new language, symbols, and myths that will allow us to discover and share a common ground. Secondly, we must change how we administer sports programs. We need to re-form sports policies and practices so that they allow for the full development of our masculine and feminine sides. We need to change how we behave as well a how we think. Most importantly, we need to be assured that if we take the first steps up the fire escape, or put another way, begin our passage across the Golden Bridge, we are not endangering ourselves, but instead are taking the first steps toward establishing a new vantage point from which to enjoy our lives together.

Hopefully, my curious grandchildren will not have to position themselves in the doorway between two rooms with the men occupying one and the women the other to be able to listen to both feminine and masculine voices, but instead share a room where they interact on a common ground. They should be able to develop both sides of their personalities, naturally, in an environment of shared interests. In certain sectors of society there is mounting evidence that at family gatherings women are less and less relegated to the kitchen. The tailgate barbecue in the stadium parking lot has become an encouraging symbol of where we are headed, with more men doing the cooking and more women venturing to express their opinions about who should be playing quarterback in the upcoming game. At a tailgate barbecue, both men and women are assembled together where there is literally no ceiling, no barriers between them as they prepare for an enlivening communal experience, where everyone, husbands and wives, boys and girls, parents and grandparents, are affirmed, uplifted, and unified by their participation in these modern day rites of enlivenment. Possibly sport can become our Golden Bridge and we can be guided by the spirit of Athena and inspired by the *Pretty Woman* myth to traverse the gap between masculine and feminine vantage points.

In the *Pretty Woman* romance-comedy one of the central characters is the hotel manager, Bernard Thompson, who serves as a mentor to "Miss Vivian," as he calls her, and as a facilitator for the

Edward-Vivian relationship. Perhaps one of the opportunities that presents itself to those of us who wish to facilitate relationships between individuals with different standpoints on sport is to position ourselves in the Doorway so that we can interpret to men and women how the other is viewing the world. Furthermore, the Doorway is not only a good place to be if one wishes to understand what men and women have to teach one another. In times of earth shaking change doorways allow one to be relatively safe from the consequences of radical shifts in the ground upon which we stand to view the world. There is no doubt that life in the Doorway can be lonely, painful, and confusing, but at the same time the door's framework can shelter one during turbulent times. Ultimately, through ceaseless effort it will be possible to break down the wall between the two rooms, eliminating not only the Doorway, but also any barriers that stand between the masculine and feminine sides of the house. Care must be taken not to do violence to any of the features of the house that deserve preserving. Both the tough and the tender are essential if men and women are to realize their full potential.

In *Pretty Woman* the tension between the masculine and feminine principles, between the tough and the tender, was reflected in the gentle battles raging in that glorious Beverly Wilshire luxury suite. The movie is fantasy, but in fact, real people experience that same tension every day in the workplace, the bedroom, and even in the gymnasium. No matter where we find ourselves the battle rages on. It is an unavoidable fact of living in the '90s in America. Sensitive artists as well as observant social critics keep the issue alive in our everyday life. But what are the origins of this battle; where is it going? In part, its roots reside in the fact of existence. Regardless of the culture in which men and women find themselves there has always been a tension between the masculine and the feminine, but at no time in history has the tension been greater than in America in the '90s. The form the tension takes at any one point in time is dependent upon the economic, political, and social context in which the "battle" occurs. Therefore, if one wishes to understand why it is happening, how it might be intelligently managed, and how to chart a reasonable course of action, then it is essential to look for answers both within ourselves and in the American culture.

There are two places where one can look to discover the roots of one's gender identity and hence one's athletic identity, the family dynamic and the social and cultural context in which one finds one-self. Let's look first at the family dynamic.

One of the most powerful social connections that affects how we relate to the masculine and feminine is our ties to our mothers. Our relationship with her is critical to how we get launched as men and women. She sets the stage for the gender battles that lie ahead. Girls and boys experience the struggle for independence and identity differently. If the psychoanalytic tradition has validity, our identity as sexual beings are all tied up in the family drama being played out between mother, father, sons, and daughters.

But the family drama occurs on a stage or a context. One must understand the impact of this context on how the family dynamic is played out. Early in each young person's life the values, language, and artifacts of the world of sport, that derive from the Culture of Conquest, begin to interact with the family dynamic. Sport is one way for parents to go beyond blue booties and pink booties in separating boys and girls. Sport is not a peripheral factor in the lives of most boys and girls growing up in contemporary America. The relationship between having balls and being given balls, instead of dolls, is established early in life. Balls, then, in both of its meanings become a significant symbol of the Culture of Conquest. When one asserts "Does he (or she) have balls!" signals that this person has the courage to take risks, to defend himself or herself against assaults from outside. One way to think of balls is that they are sources of courage and one's identity as a warrior on the playing field. The linkage between masculinity, sport, and a combative spirit is made on the day of birth when Uncle Jim delivers a football to his newborn nephew. This is the child's first induction into the Culture of Conquest. Also, "Balls, balls cried the Queen, if I had two I'd be King" was one of the early limericks I learned on the Dingle Elementary School playground as a part of my socialization into the male culture in the late '30s. "Balls," gender, courage, and privilege get closely associated early in life.

However, today the connection between "balls" and gender is more muddled. While little girls are still dressed in pink, it is not uncommon for girl babies to receive a ball, athletic shoes, or a sweat suit as a welcome into the world. As a matter of fact, as a gesture of our commitment to sport in the lives of women, our family routinely gives girl newborns a piece of athletic gear. We do this as a way of inviting them into our special culture of sport. They do need access to sport and other traditional male experiences so that they can develop the courage to prosper in competitive situations. We are always hopeful that in one of their early battles between the masculine and the feminine that girls in this New Generation will be allowed to venture out and embrace balls to their bosoms. While it is outrageous for women to artificially enhance their testosterone levels with drugs, balls, sport, and courage can become natural features of the common ground upon which men and women build their lives together.

I find it interesting that while there are people who give little girls balls to signal that it is OK to cross the Golden Bridge to the Culture of Conquest, we seem to be a long way from giving little boys dolls that would give them permission to begin thinking of themselves as caretakers, as trainees in the Culture of Care. At this point there seems to be only one way passage down the mythical path to wholeness. Are we dealing here with a taboo, on the order of the taboo in adult movies that allows woman-on-woman sex to orgasm, but absolutely no men-on-men contact. Are mothers and dads really fearful that their sons will turn into homosexuals if they play with dolls? Is this just one more example of the homophobia the feminists insist on bringing to our attention? Of course, its OK for boys to play with "dolls of terror," but not dolls of care. Once again—yes to violence, no to intimacy.

In spite of these inconsistencies it is difficult to deny that the climate in which girls and boys are inducted into their sex roles is changing. The differences we are observing cannot be attributed to significant transformations in family dynamics, but must be understood as changes in the social requirements of our times. Given the role of women in the workplace today, it is important for them to have "balls," that is, for them to adopt many traditional masculine qualities in order to be productive and survive in the rough and tumble world of corporate America. Women can, if they are en-couraged, learn some of these masculine qualities on the playing field, hopefully without doing violence to the core of their feminine values of care. More and more boys are engaged in babysitting in their free time. That too is an optimistic sign.

While we are experiencing radical changes in all sectors of our lives, a constant in all of this is that mothers continue to play the central role as caretaker and nurturer for both boys and girls. This pattern

persists, in spite of those high profile 'Mr. Moms' that have dramatically been called to our attention. These role reversals are extremely
rare. The psycho dynamics between mother and son and mother and
daughter have remained relatively constant over time. Human sexu-
ality defiantly resists being factored out of the gender identity for-
mula. This would come as no surprise to Dr. Freud. Therefore, any
social policies and practices need to reflect the very real fact of competition within the family for the affections of members of the opposite sex.

Shere Hite in her studies of men show that most boys, between the
ages of eight and 14, go through a stage of learning which involves
forcing themselves to disassociate from, stop identifying with their
mothers.

They are forced by the culture to "choose," to identify henceforth only with things
"male," not to retain any "female" ways about them, for this would "ruin their
chances" in life. This is a period of great stress for boys, who often feel guilty and
disloyal for thus "leaving" the mother; many never recover fully.[1]

She continues by concluding that boys go through four stages:
first, they identify with their mothers; then they begin to disassociate
themselves from them; next they poke fun at things feminine; and
finally they dominate the women in their lives, including their mothers, with "no qualms." This scenario demonstrates the confluence of
the family dynamic and the Culture of Conquest. Boys begin by
wanting to be "with" their mothers, but their mothers and the culture
tell them "no way." This process creates a lot of guilt on the part of
young boys. How do they learn to cope with their feelings of wanting their mothers, while at the same time separating from them and
being taught to dominate them? Boys do this by developing the
capacity to "not see" what is happening to the women in their lives,
according to Hite. The Culture of Conquest schools them on how to
put on blinders; and manly sport provides the mentoring for accomplishing this task. Edward in *Pretty Woman* was a classic case of a
man who had not resolved the conflicts that arose from the interaction of the family dynamic and the Culture of Conquest. He appeared
to have not only learned to dominate his mother, but by initiating a
corporate takeover he had been able to "defeat" his father. He was the

ultimate winner. The achievement values of the Culture of Conquest were used by him to give direction to his life. But he failed to be able to establish intimacy with anyone. His relationships with women were a disaster.

In short, there are two places one can look to discover the roots of one's gender identity, and hence one's athletic identity, family dynamics and the social and cultural context in which one finds oneself. First of all, let's look at family dynamics. One's love affair with sport is affected in one form or another by the family drama. For many boys sport is used as a way to compete with and/or bond with their fathers. At some point sport allows some of them to defeat their fathers. Or sport can be used by girls as a way of competing with their mothers for their father's attention. Or sport can be a vehicle for either competing with or bonding with the mother, if the mother is a sports activist. In any case, sport can be injected into the dynamic in ways that place it at center stage, right alongside Oedipus and Electra. But at the same time sport is a way for boys and girls to connect with the larger social community, by giving them entree into the Culture of Conquest.

In some cases sport becomes a way to escape trouble in the family dynamic, to remove oneself from the pain that results from conflicted mother-child or father-child relationships. Sport is more than a pastime. It is both a place where the family drama is enacted and a stage upon which powerful forces in the culture compete. Both of these elements, family history and cultural expectations, are internalized in the form of "voices" that guide our thinking and actions. I like the notion of hearing voices, not only because it allows one to visualize parents and others who have written a person's script standing in the wings prompting them as they make important life decisions. But I also like to use the reference to "voices" because of the association of hearing voices with madness. The tension and confusion between the voices of the scriptwriters can drive a person crazy, figuratively and literally.

When we face day to day decisions about how to live our lives, these persistent voices speak to us from the deep recesses of our unconscious. Our family's voices are always loud and clear, we generally know how they want us to respond. And the voices we have internalized from "out there" in the Culture of Conquest and the Culture of Care speak to us as well. Direction, then, comes not only from the script of the family drama, but also from the injunctions from the sub-cultures to which we belong. Mom and dad are not the only ones writing our script.

In this era, the media—TV, newspapers, magazines, and the tabloids—play a big role is establishing our expectations for ourselves and for others. No one knows for sure how powerful these prominent forces are in shaping our perspectives on gender and sport, but we can be assured that they are becoming more and more central in determining the expectations that young boys and girls set for themselves and others. We are told time and again, using the most sophisticated dramatizations and MTV media messages, how we, as men and women, are supposed to respond in all manner of situations. But the directions we get are confusing. More and more frequently the voices are not clearly heard, or they are muddled, or very likely they are in competition with one another. One voice tells young girls "fight" and the other says "yield." All of these voices have to be reconciled with one's own voice, that is, with one's core self. An important exercise for all of us, young and old, is that from time to time we need to inventory the persistent voices we are hearing to try to ascertain just how potent each is in shaping our attitudes toward work, loved ones, and ourselves. I am not calling for psychoanalytic exploration, for that is neither feasible, nor is it desirable in all cases. What I am suggesting is an exercise where each of us is encouraged to revisit the major actors in the drama of our lives, those persons who have been in a position to shape our perspectives on gender and sport. As I have learned through preparing the autobiographical materials reported in the next chapter, this personal journey can help everyone come to a better understanding of how ones values, attitudes, and ideas on sport and gender have come into being and how they impact our daily lives. By engaging in this exercise we are better able to determine whether sex role identity and our athletic identity have taken on our own special imprint or whether we are blindly following a course of action over which we exercise little control. This I call a self-estrangement check. Through some serious introspection we can determine whether it is really we who are acting or whether we are just going through the motions in response to the injunctions from our inner voices. By examining the roots of the voices one hears when one makes decisions, a better understanding can be reached about one's attitudes toward sport and gender. Is it you who is in control of your destiny, or are the voices out of your past charting your course?

CHAPTER FIVE

Journey from the Outback of Male Consciousness

... the man who integrates his feminine self becomes more
wholly masculine because he is all that he is.

Daphne Rose Kingma

I offer the story of my long, and sometimes halting, "journey from the outback of male consciousness" as an example of how such an adventure can lead to a better understanding of the origins of one's perspective on sport and gender. Hopefully, my story will inspire men and women alike to undertake their own exploration, where they can achieve a better understanding of how their standpoint came into being. I, like many men in the '90s, have been engaged in the process of sifting through the rubble of the genderquake for artifacts of civilization that can be used as a basis for building a more just world. Daphne Rose Kingma in *The Men We Never Knew* understands how men have been struggling with the challenges of the day:

The truth is that, although some men are exploring their sensitivity through therapy or men's groups, most men are still stranded in the outback of male consciousness and have miles to go before they meet women on the common ground of the conscious feminine.[1]

I no longer feel stranded in the outback, for I have quickened my pace in search of a common ground and have been able to look back and celebrate the progress I have made. I have learned that in some respects a true common ground may simply be a mirage, because the world can never look the same from different standpoints along the road to wholeness. Men and women may be traveling the same road, but they come from different points of origin. However, it seems important to remain on the road, for the closer we come to crossing paths the better view we have of one another. It has been my experience that the closer I get to the Other, the faster my heart beats, the more empowered I feel, and the more my relationships with both men and women are enlivened.

While I was a depression baby, the roots of my perspective on gender and sport can be found far before my birth, shortly after the Civil war. My paternal grandfather was born in frontier California in the late 1870s and was a young man at the turn of the century. Times were tough. He experienced the San Francisco earthquake at age 28 and participated in the rebuilding of that devastated city. Those experiences of hardship, along with a strong entrepreneurial Protestant ethic, governed his outlook on life. Not a day went by that he did not begin with the ritual of hard manual labor in his yard before going to work at the office.

As I was growing up he played an important role in my life. He and my grandmother lived in the country a few yards from my birthplace, and for the first four years of my existence were a part of my daily life. It was there that he began to impart to me his 19th century frontier ethic, which I heard as "family, family, family—work, work, work." Everyday I still hear that strong voice the moment my feet hit the floor. He was also a voracious reader, even though he only had a grade school education. He claims he was "booted out of school" for being a troublemaker. Maybe it was because he only had a grade school education that he used his latter years to compensate for his sense of loss. That I was near the completion of my Ph.D. the year he died at age 84 gave him great satisfaction. I guess I should not be surprised when the first thing I do each morning when I get up is to start the day by reading. Or that the days that give me the greatest satisfaction are those when I am free to read.

He also helped shape my ideals about family life. Every Sunday, after church, our family would gather at my grandparent's home for dinner. The gathering would always include my nuclear family plus my aunts, uncles, and cousins whenever they were in town. Hardly a day went by when I did not have an occasion to connect in some way with my grandparents. Being at their home was a very comfortable environment, so when I wanted to escape from the pressure of my parents' high achievement expectations and perfectionism, they were always there. All I had to do was call and they would come by and pick me up. (After age four we moved into town, about three miles from the family home in the country.) The commitment to family values, which meant to us investing heavily in maintaining connections with family, was firmly established in those early days. Nearly every day we are in contact by phone or in person with our children, our mothers, or our sisters, and we monitor closely the activities of all members of our extended family.

This family ideal has shaped my view of what a sports activity ought to be. It has caused me to believe that the ideal sports experience should provide the same type of sanctuary from the struggles of everyday life, as does the ideal family. The ideal sports activity should provide opportunities for participants to be refreshed and recharged before returning to take on the challenges of everyday life. The ideal family, where everyone is unconditionally committed to supporting one another through good times and bad, is one of the metaphors that guides the construction of the sports reforms we have initiated.

I deeply loved my grandparents and I cherish their memory. Very frequently more than 36 years after my grandparents died images of them pass through my mind. As a child I can remember crying myself to sleep while lying in the bedroom next to theirs, listening to their every breath, praying that these elderly "soul mates" would survive the night. I was blessed, they remained in my life until I was in my late '20s.

My grandfather never took time for sport, even though he had an athletic frame and was nearly six feet two inches tall. He had to work, not only to support his family, but also to pave the way for his salvation, as was the case for so many folks of that era who had their roots in the Protestant ethic. He frequently came to watch me compete and was supportive of my efforts, but I always had the feeling that he thought I was "playing" when I was engaged in serious training for my sports career, not "working." To this day when I go to the tennis court or take time out to watch a Rockets game, I can hear his faint voice reminding me that I should be somewhere else "doing something constructive." His voice is one of the forces that shaped my character. I have not yet been able to exorcise the demonic aspects of these memories. He is clearly sitting beside me at this moment while I am "working" at the computer, cheering me on. Time out for a high five! He is not as congenial a companion when I visit the Compact Center to witness a Rockets game. No high fives there. My outlook on sport has been greatly impacted by Gramp, even though I cannot remember one conversation we had that focused specifically on sport. His life sent me the message.

He would be pleased to know that the next generation, that included my father, carried forward these 19th century Protestant values, often times with a vengeance. No boozing, no wild women, and lots and lots of work. But there has always been room for good family fellowship, sometimes, I imagine too much. By many peoples standards, especially those of the MTV generation, that doesn't sound like much fun. He, however, established the foundation for my attitudes toward sport, my identity as a man, and my commitment to family values. He taught me that the highest virtues are work and family loyalty; that it's OK for men to read; that it's enlivening to dream; that it's splendid to have a wife who shares with her husband traditional manly duties; that a man can be kind and gentle; that there is never the need to be macho; and that women make wonderful partners in life who can share traditional male and female responsibilities.

It should not be surprising that my dad was a family man and an incurable workaholic. A very successful one I might add. He, in all that he did, echoed the voice of his father. "Work is virtue, family is everything. Sloth and infidelity are sins." He began his career as an entrepreneur in quite a remarkably fashion when he was in his early teens, partnering with his grocer uncle, in the raising of a herd of hogs. He raised them, his uncle sold them. It should have been no surprise that he ended this career as a very successful businessman and community leader. He, like his father, was the product of his era and also the creation of a family dynamic that put him in serious competition with his father and his younger sisters for his mother's affections. He entered young adulthood in the depression years. This profoundly exacerbated his tendency toward compulsive work. Survival in those desperate days depended upon keeping your "nose to the grindstone" as he was fond of saying. His attitudes toward sport and gender were products of his family situation and his times. Because he had to work throughout high school, he had little time for sport. He played on his school basketball team, but had to limit his investment in sport because of his work responsibilities.

When I entered the world of sport he was insistent that I be free to pursue sports excellence. He did not see sport as "play" as his father had, but as a way to work one's way into the public spotlight, hence facilitating a career in business. Prior to each game he came home and cooked me an appropriate pre-game meal. He supported my every move as an athlete, paying for my college tuition even when a scholarship to Stanford was offered, $200 per quarter in 1950! He missed not a single home game in eight years of high school and college, traveling to most away games as well. When I hear his voice, he is telling me that sport is "good preparation for life." It is a naive voice, in that there is little evidence that sport by itself will live up to his expectations as a vehicle for social and economic mobility. But my interest in sport as "preparation for life" undoubtedly has its roots with my depression-scarred father.

My father's relationship to women was more complicated. It was obvious that he spent his whole life proving to his mother that he was worthy of her love, just as most men do. He looked after his sisters when they were in school, even going so far as to buy up votes for his oldest sister so that she could win the campus queen title at her junior college. He was the consummate "Big Brother." As his father aged he took that same attitude toward him, looking after his every need, but keeping him in a state of dependency. He triumphed in the same way that Edward did in *Pretty Women*. He was happiest when he was able to publicly demonstrate that his accomplishments allowed him to help others. His help, however, was always awarded on his terms. He needed to be in control. He finally accomplished what Freudians would claim as the ultimate conquest. He structured it so that his father was dependent on him. Also he worked hard to get the women in his life to be dependent upon him.

My mother fulfilled his image of the traditional woman of that era. She embodied all of the classic feminine qualities, beauty, charm, and grace. She was also affectionate, passive, and fearful, and on some occasions manipulative. Like nearly all housewives of her generation she was never involved in any way with his business interests or local politics, and she had no interest, whatsoever, in family finances.

My father worked at establishing "feminine," qualities in my younger sister. She was never urged by either my father or mother to model herself after my father's "all-purpose" mother, nor was she encouraged to engage in sports, even though she was six feet tall with an athletic frame. In those days girls were taught to avoid being thought of as tough or "manly."

It would not be surprising for a son who experienced the frustration of living with a mother who lacked confidence in her abilities to vow never to choose a traditional dependent partner. When I observed how my father had perpetuated my mother's dependency, and when I experienced the pain of living with a mother who had little confidence to make decisions on her own, I was determined to partner with an independent woman. In our small town I found the most independent woman available.

Early in my life I had developed somewhat traditional expectations of a wife—there were few alternative models. The process of separating from my mother, and a small town induction into the Culture of Conquest, conspired to create some very traditional conceptions about the role of a wife. The '30s and '40s bred few men who embraced today's feminist agenda. The ideal of my grandmother was much more attractive than the ideal of my mother, however. And the fact that my aunts were working mothers gave me a glimpse of what was to come. Furthermore, the attitude of my grandfather toward my grandmother was more appealing than the attitude of my father toward my mother. Even when I was a boy of 15 my grandparents' relationship seemed better. It was then that I decided I wanted Bernice to be my partner in life. We waited six years before marrying at age 20. During that waiting period I began the long recovery from my solution to the family drama and my socialization into the Culture of Conquest. It has been a slow, tedious process that continues to this day. Full recovery may be only the dream that drives my women's advocacy efforts. I'm sure that guilt factors heavily into the explanation of my current life course; guilt that derives from a failure to truly understand and appreciate the way my sometimes dominate, condescending, and insensitive actions have impacted the women in my life—my grandmothers, mother, sister, wife, and daughters, even my female students.

I recall a time 25 years ago when I was provoked to caution a graduate student that if she pursued a Ph.D. she could be compromising her chances of developing a long-term relationship with a man. I boldly pointed out the "fact" that there are very few men who have the ego strength to partner with a highly educated woman. Even though this was in the context of a career counseling session, where I was expected to point out the costs and benefits of each of her options, my response can be understood for what it was, exceptionally sexist and totally inappropriate. Fortunately, she paid me no heed and completed her degree. She now serves as a highly successful university provost! I guess "no harm, no foul." Whether she developed a long term relationship with anyone male or female is totally irrelevant. I hope my feminist and lesbian friends will understand my transgression for what it was, insensitivity born out of ignorance.

This woman was also the insightful person who pointed out in another session, later in her graduate career, the inconsistencies in my style of leadership. She observed that I showed evidence of being comfortable with the values of the Culture of Care by always being interested in and available to my students. She recognized that I genuinely cared. But she pointed out that when I allowed the values of the Culture of Conquest to rule, my high standards of performance sometimes put a tremendous burden on the students. She observed that this tendency interfered with our relationship. That 19th century "all work, no play," approach to life was just too oppressive for her tastes. My encounters with this able and insightful woman occurred five years after I had written my first article pointing out the disadvantages women experience in our educational system!

It has been a slow road to recovery. Every day I hear voices from the Culture of Conquest, led by the baritone voice of my father, driving me "to be the best that I can be." I am prone to allow my achievement drive to interfere with my ability to get within the frame of reference of the women closest to me. Fortunately, their development is more advanced than mine and they regularly remind me of what I am doing. The loud and clear message from our daughters is not subtle, "Practice what you preach, Dad." My wife's message is more subtle, but every bit as clear. We learned our marital script when we were very young and have been practicing and regularly rewriting it for over 45 years. The process of rescripting is a most difficult challenge. Both actors in the drama have to rewrite their roles. Sometimes I have been a "slow study." Sometimes a change upsets the balance of power and neither of us is comfortable. I find it really hard to quit trying to "fix" everything, when all that these hard working women want after a "bad day at the office" is someone to listen to them and confirm that they have the ability to solve their own problems. My early experiences with a dependent mother and the Culture of Conquest did not prepare me well for life in the '90s living in a family with three independent women.

The fact that my father displayed interest in things feminine, music and dance, allowed me to understand, early on, that a man can show an interest in the genteel things in life and still be a real man. He also was a hunter who enjoyed going on trips into the wilderness with the "boys." However, even though he was formerly a trucker, he felt no need to be macho or crude. To the contrary, he was a gentle and generous man, who tried hard to be kind to everyone. He had a marketing personality so it was important for him to leave a good impression. That's good for business. "Never say anything bad about anyone, and it will never come back to haunt you," was his credo. For him it was really important to be a "nice guy." Further, he assumed leadership in his community, heading fundraising drives for the YMCA, the church, the hospital; being elected president of the chamber of commerce and the Rotary club before his 30th birthday; and serving a number of terms on the school board, much to my chagrin as a youngster. He was attentive and genial with women, but tended to want to control conversations with them. This complex man was rooted in both the Culture of Conquest and the Culture of Care, but his achievement drive, perfectionism, and need to control always dominated his decisions. His voice stands out in the chorus that informs my thinking about sport and gender.

Unlike so many professional men, I cannot identify a mentor who helped shape the direction of my life. There were men who came into my life at different points, but I never developed enough intimacy with any of them so that I feel their presence when I make significant decisions, professional or personal. Whenever I worked with a senior colleague we nearly always shared an interest in sport and a commitment to equality in relationships with women. Behavioral scientists tend to be that way. Feminism and liberalism are normative in the social science community, and many of my colleagues were dogmatic in their adherence to the principles of equality, until, of course, it came to hiring and promoting women faculty members. However, all of these mentors shared one basic Culture of Conquest quality. They were all driven to excel in their fields, to be among the top experts in their little niche of their discipline, otherwise they would not have been employed at universities that use a merit system to recognize faculty.

Turning now to the women in my life who helped shape my outlook on sport and gender I would like to focus upon my grandmothers, both of whom were central figures in my early life, both died when I was in my middle 20s. They were very much a part of my daily life while growing up. They had one quality in common, unconditional love and unqualified confidence in me to exercise good judgment. That felt real good. My grandmothers helped me develop a very positive attitude toward women. They were fun to be around and they were always there when I needed them. They never wanted me to be something I never was, and they always celebrated even my most modest achievements. When I said, "look at me," they always did, even when I did something goofy, or maybe especially when I did something goofy. They taught me that women can be fun, warm, and helpful. Even when Gram caught me sneaking a peek at her when she was undressed, she did not make me feel guilty. Everything I did seemed natural to her. How wonderful it was. No wonder I asked to go to "the ranch" every time I could. Grandparents can always do things for children that parents have difficulty doing. They generally play different roles in the family structure.

While these two women shared an enthusiasm for their first grandchild, they were very different. Gram, my father's mother, was an all-purpose woman. She ignored gender boundaries and took on all manner of tasks. She was probably the most influential person in establishing my identity. I spent a lot of time as a young boy with this remarkable women who shattered all of the conventional sex role stereotypes of her day. She was born in Victorian times of early California homesteaders. Her parents traveled across the plains in covered wagons shortly after the California Gold Rush. She loaned me her crystal clear lenses that allowed me to view the world from her remarkable perspective. She offered me, not only skill training in both traditional male and female domains, but also extended to me unconditional positive regard. This very special woman considered no task inappropriate for a woman. While most women of her day would wait until their husbands returned from work to make home repairs, she would undertake, on her own, any project with enthusiasm and skill. It is from her that I learned woodworking, painting, wallpapering, plumbing, gardening, etc. And it was also from her that I learned cooking, canning, sewing, knitting, crocheting, rug making, and housekeeping. Since I chose a life's partner who embodies these androgynous qualities, I have been reminded each day that traditional sex role stereotypes do not need to limit one's actions.

Grandmother, my mother's mother, on the other hand, was a prim and proper Victorian woman. She was widowed before I was born and lived out her life as a traditional church-going homemaker. While she went to church every Sunday, she confided to me when I was a teenager that she did not believe in an afterlife. Nevertheless, she lived her life according to Christian principles, with great kindness and care. But she was not an adventurer. She did only those things that she was comfortable with. My father looked after her financial affairs after her husband died, just prior to my parents' wedding in 1930. She had married a man 14 years her senior and was always very dependent upon him. I never knew David Canning, for he died before I was born. But I am reminded of him and his relationship to sport through an 1888 team photo of him with the "Marysville Base Ball Club" that hangs in my office. I remember hearing from both my grandmother and my mother two things about him. First of all, he was a very gentle man, not at all macho. Also I learned of his passion for baseball, a sport he enjoyed throughout his entire life, either as a player or as a spectator. When my mother was a pre-teen, he took her to the ballpark to witness a game each Sunday after church. Without question the image that my grandmother and mother created of him has impacted my identity both as a man and as an athlete.

After David Canning died my grandmother was dependent on my father for the next 26 years. She went from dependency upon her husband to dependency upon her son-in-law. She was a traditional woman for her times.

Both of these grand "ladies" born far before the turn of century were deeply rooted in the Culture of Care. That's where they achieved their identity. But my father's mother gave me a glimpse of what a woman could be. She profoundly influenced my attitudes toward women. When I was a tall gangly kid of about 10, I learned an important lesson while teasing her. She responded to my silly behavior by playfully taking me to the floor where she sat on me, pinning my arms above my head. She was then in her late '50s. That sent me several messages. Women can be spirited and fun. Never, never, underestimate a woman. And most importantly, don't mess with Gram! Forrest Gump might add, "Old is, what old does." All of those understandings have served me well throughout my life, and have shaped my expectations for women. Neither of my grandmothers figure in my athletic identity. For them it was a nice wholesome activity for their hyperactive grandson. I do not hear their voices when I step into an arena. But

I do see their images clearly when I think about how women can lead their lives.

My mother contributed to my perspective on sport in a number of ways. First of all, it was her interests in the arts, especially music and dance that established my aesthetic sensibilities. Her passion for good music and dance and her insistence on exposing me to what were at that time, in small town America considered "sissie" interests, set the stage for my initiatives to employ aesthetic metaphors in thinking about sport. (See my forthcoming book, *Change the Game: Reshaping Sport for Tomorrow's Men and Women*.) Without my mother's dedication to the arts and her persistent efforts to ensure that I developed aesthetic capabilities my enjoyment of sport would have been severely limited.

While opening up new horizons for me my mother also sent other messages that impacted my perspective on sport. When I was growing up, it seemed that so many things I wanted to do, like play with the kids in the neighborhood beyond curfew, or not do, like practice the piano, provoked a response from my mother designed to create guilt. She was very successful in that role. When I chose to play sports, she thought it would be better if I were to practice the piano or do my homework. She discouraged me from playing football beyond grade school—too brutal. It would not be surprising to expect that her voice can be heard when I participate in any sports related event, even to this day. She also got very nervous watching me compete and wore holes in her gloves from anxious fidgeting with her fingers. She was somewhat successful in transferring her stage fright to me. She still, to this day, in her early '90s, wonders how I can give public speeches and take the risks of embarrassing myself. She projects her lack of confidence on all of her intimates. She has always been both very fearful, focused on her own needs, and unsure of herself. Everything that goes on "out there" beyond the boundaries of her self needs to be connected with her personal experiences. She frequently observes, "I could never do that." It is impossible for her to identify with confident women. She considers competent women who venture into a man's world as being not very "lady like."

There is no doubt that I was attracted to my wife because she represented a more adventuresome approach to being female. Not only is Bernice different from my mother in that she is independent, assertive, and a risk taker, but she is short, when my mother is tall;

blond when my mother is brunette; slender when my mother is not; experimental when my mother is cautious.

In sum, my mother unwittingly influenced my choice of a mate and was an inspiration to me to find ways that would prevent women from being disadvantaged as she had been by her lack of self-confidence. She was the victim of a personal history that caused her to move from an older dotting father, who was nearly 50 when she was born, who responded to her every wish, to a husband who needed to keep her dependent in order to remain in control. Many of my mother's traits can be understood as a response to my father's efforts to keep her in a state of dependency in order to satisfy his own need to be in control. While growing up, I am sure my behavior did nothing but reinforce in my mother the very patterns of behavior I found frustrating. Like all family dynamics the needs of various family members tend to feed off one another.

I want to give my mother credit for the passion I possess about providing empowerment opportunities for women. If my mother's life had been different, I may not have been so driven to engage in women's sports advocacy work. I was moved by her painful experiences. Why am I doing this kind of work? I am sure that in the depths of my unconscious I am healing a deep seated childhood wound.

The "anger script" I learned in my home has affected my perspective on sport more than anything else. Unlike most boys, whose scripts allowed them to express anger as they are growing up, my script was (and still is) clearly feminine. In our culture it is expected that girls and women will deny anger in order to maintain interpersonal harmony in the home. My mother's response to outbursts of anger was to express dramatic disapproval through her actions. It was always necessary for me to initiate a reconciliation with her to end her silent disapproval when I openly expressed anger. This resulted in a "tip toe" pattern of relating to her, which still characterizes the way I act in her presence. Its the same pattern, I've just gotten better at it. I have chosen to tiptoe around her, being careful not to express my true sentiments for fear it might provoke her disapproval. I learned to address her agenda, on her terms, but not to express my true feelings, especially if they are filled with anger.

My experiences with my mother have influenced four important dimensions of my perspective on sport. First of all, I have been able to develop an aesthetic appreciation for sport that has greatly enriched my life and has influenced my sports advocacy positions. This I consider one of the most precious gifts I received growing up in my family.

Secondly, I am calling for a kinder and gentler approach to sport, where respect is shown all participants in the sports drama. This outlook has allowed me to receive the enthusiastic support of many athletes, coaches, and parents in the sports world who are uncomfortable with the direction the mainstream sports culture is taking. Kindness implies that one does not physically or verbally "tee off" on anyone, for it might hurt their bodies or their feelings. This feature of my perspective on sport relates to the anger script that I learned from my mother.

Thirdly, I am making a pitch for an approach to sport that requires all participants to pay careful attention to the agenda of the Other. In short, I am recommending that everyone show respect for the other participants, by creating "I-Thou," rather than an "I-It" relationships with the Others on the sports scene. The roots of the word respect are in the Latin word *respectus* which means "looked at." I am convinced that without my experiences with my mother I may not have made the commitment to develop sports policies and practices that attend to the needs of all participants, athletes, coaches, parents, and spectators.

And finally, being witness to the ways in which my mother was limited by the gender script she learned as a child, I have become determined to diminish the impact of those residual 19th century values on the athletes of my daughter's and granddaughter's generations. New Generation sports policies and practices can allow these two generations of women athletes to establish their womanhood in ways that do not restrict their choices. It has been my belief that with a strong and caring identity today's young women will be able to teach the men in their lives how to get more out of their sports experiences. This commitment to gender equity and justice appears to have its origins, in part, in my relationship with my mother.

In my mind, there is little question about the roots of my ideas about sport. Those aspects of my perspective on sport look suspiciously like a justification for a script that my mother and father insisted that I follow. The script I learned at my mother knee is a socially acceptable pattern of conduct that has allowed me to manage in the various roles I have occupied throughout my life. That is not to say that this script has not had costs as well as benefits. But the benefits have tended to far outweigh the costs. Emotional restraint and concern for the other's agenda are rewarded handsomely in our culture, especially today in organizations that require networking in order to accomplish information age missions. Therefore, this restrained, other-centered pattern of behavior has been regularly reinforced throughout my entire life and has revealed itself in each major decision I have made. This pattern has persevered and is revealed in every sports development project I have undertaken.

There is no doubt that everyone's perspective on sport is profoundly influenced by his or her family dynamic. That is why it seems so essential to embark upon a search for wholeness, if one wishes to achieve rational control over the sports script one is following. Sometimes insights into the roots of our family dynamic will give us cause to rewrite a dysfunctional script. Other times it will give the self explorer the understanding needed to keep from engaging in excesses in the name of outdated myths. At the very least, it will provide one with the humility needed to avoid imposing one's perspective on others. Many moralists have not achieved that humility and are bound and determined to lay an angry trip on anyone whose family dynamic and life experiences do not allow them to come to the same conclusions.

This is not to say that it is impossible to discover a set of principles that are independent of a person's unique life experiences, for I think that there are some universal ethical principles. What I am suggesting is that each of us experiences life in ways that influence our choices, including our decisions about how to relate to the world of sport. We need to understand the forces that are influencing our choices. They can help us gain rational control over our lives, so that we will be better able to enjoy the opportunities that are out there, and be less frustrated when things do not go our way.

After coming to an understanding about the roots of my perspective on sport I believe I am better able to understand why most men, especially those raised before the '60s consciousness raising era, have difficulty resonating to a perspective on sport that places so much emphasis upon mutual respect and emotional control. Most men have been taught a much tougher script that allows them to freely express their anger. Therefore, they see no reason why a competitive situation, like sport, should not permit them to give vent to their feelings, whether from the sidelines or the playing field. It would seem unnatural to do otherwise. For them, it does not seem to be a big leap from having permission for the expression of anger to having permission for the expression of violence, since that is also a part of most men's scripts. They learn that manly script so that they can perform their functions as protectors of women and children. Even though male aggression may in part have its origins in higher testosterone levels and in a collective history of men having to fight with other men for sexual favors from women, the unique family dynamic that each man experiences profoundly influences the form his script takes. It all begins with "Big boys don't cry." No men want their script to end as it does in a 1994 Randy Travis ballad about a son who finds a box of mementos left by his dead father. On a top shelf he finds a collection of items that reveals a tender side of his father that had been effectively masked during his lifetime. Fathers do not want their children to sing after they are gone that, "We all thought his heart was made of solid rock."

In the case of anger control, each person can be placed on a continuum from masculine to feminine. Those who fall toward the masculine end will feel comfortable with a perspective on sport that derives from the Culture of Conquest guided by its military metaphor. Anger has served the tribe well, for it has allowed men to take actions to protect their women and children from harm. On the other hand, those who fall toward the feminine end, having been scripted to work hard to achieve interpersonal harmony, will determine that the perspective on sport that derives from the Culture of Care will "feel better." Also harmonizing has served the tribe well, for it has allowed both men and women to build unity within the family and community.

How does one go about determining which solution to the control of anger should be applied to sports policies and practices? Are the masculine and the feminine approaches equally appropriate? How does one chose how to come down on this issue? First of all, I am making a case that each person has the responsibility to come to a better understanding of the roots of his own outlook on sport. The origins of one's perspective can be found, in part, in the family dynamic and in other prominent life experiences. Secondly, one can look to the requirements of the times for guidance. Knowing what the other social institutions are asking of their participants can suggest directions for sport. And finally, but most importantly, one can search for basic moral principles to guide one's expression of anger. The universal Golden Rule seems to work for me. "Do unto others as you would have them do unto you." Most of us wish to avoid the wrath of the other players in the drama of sport, the coaches, referees, opponents, teammates, and spectators, therefore this principle would advise us to avoid venting anger on others. Such outbursts are both insensitive and disrespectful. Or one could apply Buber's notion of "I-Thou" relationships that enjoins one to be guided by fundamental respect for the other. That works for me. It never seems right to treat a person, as so many coaches are prone to do, as interchangeable objects rather than as subjects. Furthermore, if a major function of sport is to help build common bonds and a sense of community, it seems more reasonable to factor out as much anger as possible from these renewal rituals.

We should always be open to the possibility that our choice of an ideology to support our perspective is itself rooted in our family dynamic. I may very well be choosing the golden rule and the I-Thou philosophy simply to justify a pathological script. This "humane" choice makes me feel that I am traveling the high road. I'm sure that those who embrace the Lombardian philosophy feel that they are traveling a route grounded in a basic reality of human nature, that only the fittest survive. Which principle should prevail in decisions about how to treat fellow sports participants, the Golden Rule, or the Darwinian notion of the "survival of the fittest" (or in the mainstream sports lexicon, the belief that one has to "dominate or be dominated")? The answer has to be found through an examination of both the roots of one's perspective on sport and in an evaluation of the requirements of the day. Does the situation call for displays of aggression or warmth. The answer has to come from considerations of what is right as well as what works to accomplish the mission at hand. Aggression may produce winners, but the price may be too great.

The case I am making, then, is that it is essential to 1) understand how one's script got written, 2) know what the times are calling for, and 3) search for a set of moral principles that can be flexibly applied to one's day-to-day decisions in sport. These principles are essential when you "feel" like doing one thing, and the situation is telling you to do another. Both our feelings, rooted in our unique script, and the specific situational requirements, are appropriate to bring into the decision-making process. But basic principles of human decency need to play a prominent role. But if principles are applied either rigidly or blindly, without the benefit of self-knowledge and a comprehensive understanding of each situation, there is always a chance they will be misapplied.

Too frequently moralists display neither respect for their subjects, nor a comprehensive understanding of the situation in which the dilemma is occurring. For them it just feels wrong and they have little understanding of the psychological dynamics of how they arrived at their position. This is true for many of the radical feminists who vent their anger on all men, rather than trying to understand the origins of the behavior of those men who are transgressors of principles of human decency.

Since childhood, there have been many turning points in my life that have impacted significantly my attitudes about sport and gender. When I was in Korea, I took along a footlocker of books that I had always wanted to read during college. My collegiate sports training schedule gave me few hours to pursue non-course-related intellectual interests. As I was enjoying these books, I realized how my sports training had cheated me out of so many opportunities. It wasn't until my tour in Korea that I came to understand that I had attended one of the nation's finest universities, but had not taken full advantage of Stanford's vast intellectual and social resources. I realized very clearly, in that tent near the 38th Parallel, just how limiting a college sports career can be. I feel confident that this enforced retreat to peacetime Korea influenced my cautious enthusiasm for recommending college sports to either men or women.

The awakening I had when my wife discovered her undeveloped athletic potential after age 40 also profoundly affected my ideas about women and sport. And, the experiences I've had with our daughters have shaped my views and fired my passion for creating sports opportunities that truly empower women participants.

The regular conversations I have with athletes; high school, club, or college coaches; athletics administrators; referees; event managers; and members of the sporting goods manufacturing community; always remind me why I need to continue my efforts. The old male-constructed myths and folk tales are alive and well and continue to show significant resistance to change. Those voices, articulating the conventional wisdom of the Culture of Conquest, are with me constantly, as a reminder of the job that remains to be done.

John Stoltenberg in *Refusing To Be A Man* expresses his understanding of why he has made a choice to climb into the corner with
women and challenge traditional patterns of male behavior.

One of the reasons I started to care about radical feminism as much as I did was
because it seemed to resolve for me a certain dilemma about myself in relation to
other men. I had always felt irremediably different—even when no one else noticed,
I knew; I knew I wasn't really one of them....Radical feminism helped me imagine a
gender-just future, a notion of a possibility that men need not be brutish and loutish,
that women need not be cutsey and coy. It was a vision that energized me....Radical
feminism helped me honor in myself the differences that I felt between myself and
other men; radical feminism helped me know my connections to the lives of women,
with whom I had imagined I would ever find a model for who I could be. And it's also
true—and not easy to admit—that radical feminism helped provide me with a forum
in which to express my anger at other men—an anger that in men can run very deep,
as many of us know....In various ways, feminism has blown like a gust of fresh air
through a lifetime spent agonizing and anguishing about the place of other men in our
lives. For a few of us, feminism has helped us breathe a bit easier.[2]

My experiences with women in sport have not only raised my consciousness about the plight of women, but caused me to come to a
better understanding of my relationships with other men, especially
my father. His relationship with me, my mother, my sister, and later
my wife, has played a significant role in defining how I relate to
women and other men.

It is impossible to attend to my relationships with women without
being challenged to assess my relationships with men. Over the years
I have had difficulty connecting with many traditional males. I have
not experienced difficulty in getting along with traditional men, but I
have found it a challenge to get within their frame of reference. They
make me uneasy with the way so many of them treat the women in
their lives. To say the least, my integration into the Culture of
Conquest has been less than complete. I have been engaged in a lifetime of refusing, in one way or another, to be a "real man." No tat-
toos, no beard, no booze, no cigars or chewing tobacco, no poker, no
bimbos, no guns, no black labs, no tractor caps, no fist fights, no
pick-up trucks, and—few men with whom to share my life. I'm sure
"Bubba" would say, " and no fun either." Sport has been my major
bond with mainstream American men.

There have been many times when my disenchantment with the

traditions of the male culture has made me feel like an outsider. I was always unwilling to submit to the hazing one must go through in order to earn citizenship in the community of men. However, I did have good enough sports credentials to make me appear to be "one of the guys." However, I sometimes think of myself as "a nerd in jocks clothing." My disinterest in hunting and fishing, my lack of enthusiasm for tinkering with cars, my rejection of drinking parties, and my propensity for spending time with my steady girlfriend were signs of alienation from the mainstream male culture in small town America, even when I was a teenager in the '40s.

My refusal to adapt to fraternity life at Stanford after pledging as an Alpha Delt, signals my discomfort with the customs and habits of men-as-men. In my own mind, I justified withdrawing from the fraternity prior to initiation as a protest against the fraternity president's official complaint on behalf of the Stanford chapter to the University of Illinois chapter for pledging a Black. It seems clear to me, with 48-year hindsight, that my actions were also inspired by an uneasiness with the community of traditional males. The fraternity I pledged was one of the most civilized of its era, counting few jocks and many top scholars and student leaders among its members. It was surly no Animal House. Nevertheless, this able group of Alpha Delts embraced interests and values that were out of sync with those of a small town teenager who had already chosen a marital partner and who did not share either their interest in partying or their attitudes toward African Americans.

Instead, I joined the El Capitan Eating Club, that allowed me to take my meals with a group of men who did not fit the typical male pattern of the day. Among them were Jews, Blacks, Nerds (most of whom wore horn-rimmed glasses and carried slide rules on their belts), and plenty of young men who were just simply socially awkward or did not, in some way or another, fit the "real man" pattern that would allow them to fit into the fraternity mold. This eating club, which required no real social investment, was a loose federation of exceptionally interesting individuals who did not expect one another to conform to the manly image of the day. I was one of the few jocks among them. Clearly, I felt I was an outsider in the Stanford jock culture. As Soltenberg said, "even when no one else noticed, I knew; I knew I wasn't really one of them."

During my junior year at Stanford I took an apartment off-campus with one of my freshmen roommates, Joe Bacon, a wonderfully gifted renaissance man. He had been on the Stanford frosh crew when we were assigned to the same room during our freshman year. His real appeal to me was not his interest in sport, but his questioning mind and his unconventional approach to the world. He was the heir to an industrial fortune—his mother was the daughter of a leading manufacturer of bathroom fixtures. His father was the head of the music department at Yale and his mother lived with her second husband in luxury in Marin County.

I had never been around anyone like Joe who was so independent of conventional definitions of how a man ought to live his life. He played life by a different set of rules, and I admired that. I remember visiting his home and hearing his stepfather playing a Baroque instrument, the recorder, in the living room. When he was not pursuing his musical interests, he was driving his Jaguars in road races. They had a servant who served us the meals when I visited, all of the perks that go with upper class life that liberate family members from the routines of daily chores. They were truly an upper class family who had been among the privileged long enough to be able to take full advantage of the freedom it presented.

During my college years no man influenced my definition of what it meant to be a man more than Joe Bacon. Joe learned to play the classical guitar during our year together (he later studied with Andres Segovia, the great Spanish guitarist), he pursued a philosophy curriculum, and followed all of his intellectual interests without any concern what others might think of him. It seems as though the factor that bonded the two of us was that we both realized we were "different" and were struggling to find our way. He was a most resourceful guide. It was truly liberating being around him. He gave me courage and inspiration to pursue interests and issues that I had, but which I was too timid to explore. We talked for hours about ethics, psychology, and the meaning of life.

With his encouragement I enrolled in a class with Professor Reed, a psychiatrist teaching a course on the philosophy of interpersonal relations. This course impacted my life more than any other course I took during my academic life. More than 45 years later I remember in detail what I learned in that course. We studied psychoanalysts Freud, Fromm, and Horney and where required to write a paper applying their ideas to our own life experiences. It was then that I begin to understand how profoundly my father was impacting my life. My term paper was an effort to better understand our relationship. The experience of taking this course and having a curious and brilliant roommate with whom to discuss the issues not only led me to change my major to psychology, but profoundly modified the course of my life. Joe Bacon and his family modeled alternative ways of being a man that allows both the masculine and feminine sides to find expression—from road racing to Baroque music. The old money, upper class life style often encourages men to set themselves apart from the common man. Witnessing that model was liberating to me, for it seemed to fit my predisposition and my needs at that point in my life.

Throughout most of my adult life, that was spent mainly in an academic setting, I was among men who had great tolerance for different ways of playing at being a man. I frequently sought out graduate student colleagues and faculty members who found it possible to combine their commitment to liberal politics, dedication to the academic life, with an interest in sport. As a graduate student at Michigan I played on the psychology department volleyball and softball teams that included both grad students and faculty. The softball team captain and star pitcher was the distinguished scholar, Bill McKeachie, head of the department. And my closest friend in graduate school, Dick Schmuck, was an accomplished athlete, a Phi Beta Kappa in English Literature, and a political activist. The men I associated with were "real men" by anyone's standards, but they were all successful in tempering their commitment to Culture of Conquest values with genuine concern for the welfare of the disadvantaged and the disenfranchised, especially women. They all had wives who were truly partners in their families, and in some cases in their academic work. It seemed natural to further develop my commitment to improving the prospects for women when I was in their midst.

It was not until after I had left university work and returned to our rural hometown to assume responsibilities for managing family business interests (after my father had a disabling stroke) that I was rudely awakened to the realities beyond the walls of the academy. Twenty five years after graduating from high school my classmates were still relating to the women in their lives in the same manner as their fathers had before them. This was both a consciousness raising experience and a provocation for activism. I was more determined than ever that our daughters would not have to suffer the indignities and limitations I was observing in Woodland, California, in the '70s. Their mother shared my agenda and we set out with great passion to clear the pathway so that our daughters could learn the skills they needed to take charge of their lives. We encouraged them in their sports endeavors because we believed, rightly or wrongly, that sports training would prepare them for redefining traditional gender boundaries.

Experiences with my wife and daughters "helped me remember a gender-just future." My passion to effect change could not have developed to the level it has without a break with the traditional male culture. Clearly, my mother, bless her heart, has always been on the sidelines cheering on any revelation of my feminine side. Brutish and loutish men were never celebrated by either my mother, or my father, for that matter.

It has been a life-long project to come to terms with what it means to be a man. Without systematic self-exploration it is not possible to prevent one's sex role scripting from being, not only an inhibitor to growth and opportunity, but also a barrier to the development of a moral identity. Stoltenberg defines "moral identity" as being "a part of ourselves that is capable of living beyond gender." Sport cannot be allowed to prevent men and women from being challenged to develop a sense of responsibility toward all of humanity. Men and women must be encouraged to struggle with the conflict between their moral identity, their sense of fairness, and their gender identity. Our connections with other men and women make it difficult to subordinate gender identity to moral identity. That is why it is so important to eradicate sexism.

Those of us, then, who possess a less differentiated gender identity, are in an advantageous position to provide leadership for the gender transition movement. The challenge is that there are always going to be a long line of "prompters" on the sideline who will be vigorously trying to prevent us from straying from the traditional sex role course. Those who recognize how the game is being played, those who have been able to overcome their sex role scripting, need to position themselves on the sideline as close as possible to the participants so that they can hear the cheers for the triumph of the moral over the gender self. It is my experience that cheers work better than jeers to keep participants on course. That is a lesson most entrenched traditionalists and many militant feminists have yet to learn.

It is my belief that most traditionalists embracing the values of the manly culture of sport have never been provoked to examine the roots of their gender selves, nor have many of them taken a careful, systematic look at the "gender wars" that are occurring in the rest of society. Coaches and athletics administrators often have a very small window through which to view the rest of the world. Also they have not been allowed to develop fully their moral selves, that is, their sense of fairness about how men and women should be treated. Regrettably most are not prepared to guide either our sons or daughters into the 21st century.

I am reminded that the members of the sports establishment spend nearly all of their time talking among themselves and with their "recruits." It is no wonder there is a ground swell of impassioned cries among coaches about "intrusive" parents. Concerned parents are, indeed, barging in to remind coaches that we are approaching the 21st century and that the "software" they are using is not up to the task. And rightly so, for it is the children of these parents who are being denied updated treatment. More importantly, parents are living in the "real world," being reminded day in and day out just how ineptly yesterday's ways are addressing today's needs.

The gym door will have to be opened wider if the light of the 21st century is to shine in. Be assured there will be collective efforts made by sports education professionals to shut the door on input from New Generation voices. But these voices need to be heard if sport is going to be in tune with the requirements of the times. The current chorus of voices, some of which are speaking in high-pitched tones and are rooted in New Generation values, have to be integrated with both the voices of yesterday and the inner voices from newly awakened moral selves. There is often inner disharmony of a significant order. But I would be encouraged if men and women were challenged to embark upon an exploration into the recesses of their souls in search of the roots of their perspectives on sport and gender. This step, supplemented by an examination of new ideas about the role of sport, should set the stage for rescripting the drama of sport.

Sport could become a sanctuary where men and women search for wholeness. It has the potential of being a refuge where participants are free to test out different aspects of themselves, where they can count on mentors and peers to support their self-discovery efforts. If that dream can be realized, a giant step will have been taken toward transforming a historic battleground into a common ground where men and women establish a climate of creative cooperation.

Judy Mann in *The Difference* has concluded:

In their journey away from dominance, boys and men will have the opportunity to become more thoughtful of others and to learn to form the kinds of deep, relational networks that women have—the kinds of friendships that support and nourish us when careers are faltering, marriages are ending, and children are hovering on the brink of delinquency. For women, "a little help from my friends" is not an empty phrase: Often it is a rescuing lifeline. This is one of many things boys and men can learn from us. They do not deserve to be brought up in the arid emotional isolation that patriarchies inflict on them.[3]

This opportunity to move away from "arid emotional isolation" may appear to many observers, especially women, like an alternative that men would enthusiastically seek. From a woman's perspective it would seem natural for men to work to gain relief from their loneliness. Unfortunately, for men inducted into manhood in the male culture of sport, where toughness and independence are so highly prized, the journey away from dominance and isolation in most cases is torturous and frustrating. While new generation men are beginning to learn to form "deep relational networks...that nourish us," most American men still have a long way to go on their journey from the outback of male consciousness. We must not allow sport to become a barrier to achieving this humanizing and harmonizing end. We men need to listen carefully to women's voices on the playing field and in other areas of our lives. If we pay close attention to what they are saying and especially to how they are living their lives together we will hear their caring invitation to share with them the kinds of intimacy that can restore our souls when we are most in need of revitalization. Simply by listening we will have taken a giant step toward finding our way out of the outback and toward connecting with women who can help us transform sport from a masculine to a human experience.

Fortunately, not all aspects of the male world are savage. Women can benefit from visiting a challenging environment where they are allowed to enjoy being tested against those forces that are limiting their opportunities to develop into fully functioning women. It requires a certain amount of grit for women as well as men to get through the trials of competition. The tests women face as they venture out of traditional feminine roles are the same kinds of tests men face as they embark upon their pilgrimage through the outback. Equal opportunity means that women can gain access to the same benefits as men and, of course, pay the same price. Men and women learn best about how to negotiate life's challenges when they listen carefully to one another and try to give and receive helpful guidance as they progress through the life cycle. In sport, as in other sectors of life, both men and women need the support of fellow trailblazers. Men must resist, however, the temptation to take charge of their joint ventures with the women in their lives. Sharing power, we learn, is never easy.

I have found this pilgrimage into the depths of my consciousness extraordinarily demanding, sometimes overwhelming, and nearly always unsettling. The very thought of giving up control is frightening to most men, especially those of my generation, who have not been taught to share power with the women in their lives. Even New Generation men reluctantly give up their male prerogatives. More often than not, however, the new discoveries made on this journey have been uplifting and enchanting. I feel assured that it is indeed worth the investment to follow this uncharted route. I am happy to be a stakeholder in a new era in sport that gives signs of being guided by values that prize the feminine as well as the masculine aspects of our experiences on the playing field. This cultural renaissance is creating a common life where men and women are becoming partners in the quest for completion.

Casualties

CHAPTER SIX

The Game That Never Ends

*In most societies, the tests for manhood are never considered
finished; it is impossible for a man to feel that he has found a
permanent place in the community of men. He believes that he
can always slip back over the line, losing his manhood and suffering shame and disgrace by failing to meet the next test.*

Ronald F. Levant
A New Psychology of Men

Shortly before my 40th birthday my good friend,
Patrick James O'Malley (the name has been changed as have the
non-essential features of the story to protect the identity of the story's
subject), with whom I regularly played pick-up basketball at the local
sports club, underwent ankle surgery for the third time. When visiting him in the hospital I was provoked to reflect upon the role of
sport in his life, my life, and in the lives of the other men and women
I knew. It was during that visit to the hospital that I decided to take
my wife's advice and give up basketball for squash, a much more
appropriate sport for middle-aged men.

On that cold winter day, I was impressed with the fact that
Patrick's wife had refused to visit him at the hospital. She apparently was fed up with his reluctance to abandon what she referred to as
"his adolescent obsession with sport." This hospital encounter was
one of the first times I had been caused to be very reflective about
sport, which is testimony to how thoroughly many of us men have
been scripted as jocks. Sports are just something men do. Patrick's
wife's behavior, which I considered at the time to be extraordinarily
insensitive, and my wife's insistence that I change my ways, inter-
rupted my usual pattern of thinking about athletics, and brought into
sharp contrast traditional masculine and feminine perspectives on
sport. His wife, Carrie, had been reared as a traditional woman,
whose family prized intellectual and commercial, rather than athletic
success. She had chosen a feminine career, elementary school teaching, after their two sons were of school age. She had little interest in

sport, and little tolerance for her husband's obsession with sport. Her impatience with his passion reminded me once again that men and women, because of the ways they are scripted from birth, generally assign radically different meanings to these activities. Carrie had never seriously experimented with sport as she was growing up, so she was unable to share in any significant way what was one of the most central features of her husband's life. At best she was tolerant of Patrick's "addiction." She had regular access to her family and friends with whom she shared traditional feminine interests. And Patrick had his friends and business associates with whom to engage in "sports talk." This was not an unusual pattern of relationship for married couples of the Silent Generation.

As an adult Patrick played several sports on a regular basis, stopping off on his way home from work to play softball, touch football, and squash as well as basketball. By 40 he had reached the point where his fierce competitive nature was responsible for the violence being done to his body. He had a series of physical setbacks as he approached middle age, caused to a great extent by his inability to change his game to accommodate aging. He still slid hard into second base and went to the floor for loose balls on the basketball court. He was at that time, and still is for that matter, 25 years later, reluctant to shed his identity as an athlete. Interestingly, the wounds that he receives in athletic battle, while dispiriting, are, in a way, badges of courage he proudly displays. These prominent scars assure him and those around him that he is, without question, maintaining his athletic credentials. Athletes like Patrick like to think of themselves as just too tough to give up, or as they say today, "too legit to quit." Patrick is an Irish George Forman. He is determined to win in his battle with nature in the name of preserving his manly identity that derives from his participation in sport.

Each of my age peers, who has developed a strong athletic identity, has chosen some special way to preserve his connection with his past athletic achievements. Without exception, each dresses out in athletic gear at the slightest provocation. Some tell animated "war stories" about the good old days. Others find it necessary to discredit the current crop of athletes as not being as tough, disciplined, or well trained as "they used to be." When I am with these former athletes hardly a day goes by that they do not go through their particular routine that connects them to the world of sport. These retreats to their roots become rites of empowerment. It is important to Patrick and others like him for their identities as athletes to be confirmed on a regular basis.

In spite of the fact that Patrick has had a very successful career as a corporate executive, bringing him both recognition and enviable economic security, his primary identity is still that of a "jock." Like his age peers he cannot wait to get home each night and put on his athletic gear. Only when he is outfitted in sneakers and a sweatshirt, ready for battle on the playing field, does he seem to be "at home." Even though he has lived the vast majority of his life in a corporate suite, whenever he reflects upon his situation he places himself squarely in the middle of the mainstream sports culture where he is constantly affirming his worth through reporting and reflecting upon athletic events and achievements, both past and present. Sport was, and continues to be, Patrick's primary point of reference.

Growing up in an Irish Catholic parish in a big city, Patrick found his comfort level on the playgrounds. As a youngster he spent little time at home except to study and eat. His mother was a troubled woman who drank too much, making it more comfortable for him to spend as much time as possible with the neighborhood boys in the gym and on the playing field. In his youth he received much public recognition for his athletic accomplishments, winning the city high jump championship, and being named an All-State basketball player. His athletic 6'7" frame helped him earn an athletic scholarship to a selective university in the Southeast, where he became an All-Conference basketball player. This recognition got him a job with a major international import-export corporation that had historic ties with his university. He remained with that company for 35 years, retiring at age 57 as its vice president. He continues working as hard as ever as a financial consultant to his company and to other businesses with whom he has worked over the years. As he trudges off to work each day, or takes a client out for a golf outing the pain of deteriorating knees remind him of the "battles" he has waged to retain his credentials as a jock.

As I have come to get better acquainted with this exceptional man, I have been reminded, each time I am able to spend time with him, that for many American males early experiences with sport can have a profound effect on scripting the course of one's life. In Patrick's case it is unclear just how his experiences in sport influenced his career other than to get his foot in the door, and to give him some business contacts that his fleeting athletic notoriety afforded him. It is hard to sort out just how the things he learned in the gym affected his corporate career. However, in his own mind there is a very clear relationship. He is convinced that the toughness and competitiveness he learned in sports has served him well in the business world, and credits his success as an executive to the discipline and focus he learned on the court, as do other prominent achievers like former Supreme Court Justice Byron "Wizzer" White, former President Gerald Ford, former Senator Jack Kemp, and former Senator Bill Bradley. It is quite possible, however, that competitiveness, discipline, and focus are qualities these accomplished people learned in their youth that allowed them to be exceptionally successful in school, sports, and then in their respective careers. The fact remains that because of the centrality of sport in Patrick's life, it seems natural for him to connect nearly everything in his life to his core athletic self. Even after radical heart bypass surgery at age 53 he has returned to active sports competition. Nothing pleases him more today than to be able to defeat a younger man on the squash court, something his exceptional skills and long experience allow him to do from time to time. He continues to be a remarkable, driven athlete.

What about the other dimensions of Patrick's life? Has he been able to establish intimacy with the significant people in his life? Not unlike many achieving males of his era, self-disclosure and intimacy do not come easily. While he worked hard at making his first marriage a success, he was unable to develop the kind of relationship with his wife and children that allowed him to get emotionally close to any of them. In his early 40s after persistent effort, he abandoned any hope of salvaging his deteriorating relationship with his wife. That failed episode in his life, the split-up, was difficult for him to integrate with his traditional Roman Catholic family values, but more importantly with his image of himself as a good husband and father.

His loyalty to family and friends never wavered throughout his lengthy struggles with his marriage. He felt he had worked hard at being a good husband and father, but had fallen short. The fact remains there was nothing in his Irish Catholic upbringing that prepared him for getting close to anyone, his parents, siblings, wife, or children. The mainstream culture of sport, into which his sports-obsessed father inducted him, has made it difficult for Patrick and his age peers to develop their capacity to give expression to deep seated feelings. Real men take care of their own problems. Neither the board room nor the locker room are good places to share ones personal secrets, unless, of course, it is to boast of ones sexual conquests. Romantic interludes were not Patrick's ways of affirming his masculinity.

This ethic of self-sufficiency continues to this day to guide Patrick in his day to day life, and was clearly revealed recently when his teenage daughter, from his second marriage, was in need of counseling for serious personal and educational problems. He found it difficult to be a party to the therapeutic process. Self-disclosure and dependency are just not easy for men of his generation who have been socialized into the mainstream athletic culture, or for most males of any generation, even today when males are being given permission to be more open and expressive. Athletic men find it dysfunctional to reveal their weaknesses. To allow a competitor to become aware of a weakness could very well expose one to possible exploitation and eventual defeat, both on the playing field and in the corporate world.

Patrick also revealed a typical male mode of operation in the way he approached the moral dilemmas surrounding his divorce. Like most men, he justifies his behavior according to an abstract code of conduct that was scripted for him as he was growing up. It was not so much that he had adopted the Catholic Ethic about marriage and family, for he is not a very observant member of his faith. Instead, I have come to understand that early in his life he adopted a very limiting code of loyalty, which still pervades every aspect of his life, both on and off the playing field. He is a real team player. As a result of this scripting he can be counted on to be a fiercely loyal friend. He has been taught to behave according to clear principles of personal conduct. At the time of his divorce he had real difficulty taking into account the situational factors that could be used to justify the split. He kept repeating to himself and to others that it was just not right to turn ones back on one's family. He had difficulty taking into account how a change in marital status could impact, positively, the lives of the principle people in his life. Divorce was not only an admission of failure to Patrick, but also a violation of a basic ethical principle, "Thou shalt be loyal to one's friends and family." He has spent the past 15 years making dramatic gestures to assure himself and others that he has been loyal to his family. He has gone way beyond what the situation has dictated to demonstrate his commitment to his family, providing them with any support they have needed to make their lives comfortable. He gives signs of still feeling guilty about his divorce action, in spite of much evidence to indicate that everyone benefited from the change. His former wife went back to school, remarried, and occupies a leadership role in her school district. He also expresses disappointment that neither of his two sons made a significant commitment to sport. It should not be surprising that neither of his sons has chosen to compete on his father's turf. Patrick still holds out hope, however, that his young daughter will choose to develop the athletic talents she gives evidence of possessing. But at last report she was deeply entrenched in adolescent rebellion, uninterested in doing anything her family wanted.

Patrick has been scripted to develop those aspects of himself that allow him to function effectively in the world of work. He is a gentle, but ambitious, man who throughout his life has used sports as a means of affirming his self-worth. He is not only driven to achieve, but also to fulfill his responsibilities to his family and friends. While acquiring professional skills and the capacity for responsibility, like so many other men who have central athletic identities, he has neglected the development of his capacity for intimacy. He enjoys being in the presence of jocks, for they seldom place emotional demands upon him. Their "trading card culture" in which they play games such as "What did you think of the Bullets game last night?" and the many other distant-keeping routines that feed the relationships, but by their very nature discourage self disclosure and intimacy.

While Patrick has been dedicated to maintaining strong family values, his athletic focus has not allowed him to develop his capacity to get close, with anyone. He has been too competitive with males to let them in, even though he has many loyal long time friends. And he has been baffled by the women in his life. He has found it almost impossible to figure out how to get within their frames of reference. He has developed a number of recurrent games that he plays with his wife and daughter that allow him to avoid being intimate. His favorite game is to play "Big Daddy" where he looks after everyone. This game requires that he work hard to bring in plenty of money so that he can rescue anyone in distress. By yielding to his family's preferences and avoiding frequent encounters and, hence, conflict, he has been able to maintain cordial working relationships with his family.

By seeking out traditional women, as do so many men who have established an athletic identity, he has been able to continue enacting a script that maintains the status quo.

Patrick's life story is familiar to those who have looked carefully at the role of sport in the lives of men. Sociologist Michael Messner in *Sex, Violence, and Power in Sports* concludes:

My research with former athletes suggests that extreme adherence to the athletic role actually serves to exacerbate the most destructive elements of traditional masculine identity. In particular, the extreme goal-orientedness that the successful athlete adopts tends to undermine his ability to establish and maintain intimate relationships with women and with other men.[1]

Without question Patrick has problems with establishing and maintaining intimate relationships with women and for that matter with men as well. For as long as I have known Patrick he has expressed his bafflement about how to relate to women. Each time he and his female partners have attempted to rewrite their script, he has been frustrated and has regressed to traditional patterns of relationship with which he and they are comfortable. He has not allowed himself to discover those feminine possibilities that were lost through his early sex role scripting. Even family crises have not provoked situations to give him permission to open himself up to others. Please understand, he is kind, generous, and most accommodating in his relations with his wife and children. But he has great trouble, both at listening to what they are really saying, as well as at being self-disclosing, which makes genuine intimacy impossible. Also being as committed as he is to self-sufficiency, it is unlikely that he will seek out professional assistance to find that part of him that has been lost. If one does not know what to look for, it is difficult to find it. Certainly he will not find those undeveloped aspects of himself in sports without completely transforming his approach to that enterprise. He has little incentive to do that, since the endless psychological games he plays are comforting and self-perpetuating. It is most likely that Patrick will continue to be the Big Daddy that everyone admires and respects, but no one really knows. He is playing a game that never ends. Hopefully, the New Generation sons of the Big Daddys of contemporary America are learning how to be men without paying the price their father's have had to pay.

It will be difficult for Patrick's sons to learn a new game until such time that the women in their lives cheer for tender men who listen rather than for the men who have become their objects of success. Also, if change is to occur men must actively protest against being chosen by women for their ability to win in their "conquests" out there in the "real world" rather than for their ability to provide emotional nurturance. Those who care about Patrick and his "brothers" can ease their suffering by refusing to support Culture of Conquest myths that prevent the development of the latent nurturer-connector that resides deep within the souls of all men. The millennium in sport cannot be reached without a heightened awareness of the impact of sport on the lives of those who have been socialized into the Culture of Conquest, or without the courageous and patient collaboration of the women in their lives, their mothers, sisters, wives, partners, and workmates.

Daphne Rose Kingma in *The Men We Never Knew* has concluded:

Men are still in the boondocks emotionally, not because women have failed them in the past, but because only now has the sociological and emotional climate matured to the point where this transformation can occur at a conscious, premeditated level. Now is the time to begin. Time for women to get on the job of initiating certain behaviors, and a time for men to learn the precepts, language, and behaviors that will develop their relationship capacity.[2]

I like to think it is not too late for Patrick, me, or the rest of our brothers to cease playing the games we have learned all too well over the years. A new set of rules can be written and we can all become players in a new social order in which the games we play liberate us from the constraints of our upbringing rather than further entrench us in traditional sex role niches.

Creative Tension

CHAPTER SEVEN

So, Do Women Hate Baseball?

Because of traditional patterns of child rearing sport has come to be much more central to a man's identity than to a women's. This is nowhere more clearly represented than in the movie *City Slickers* featuring Billy Crystal's character and his New York buddies who have joined a cattle drive in New Mexico to "find themselves." Among others, they are joined by a young woman whose apparent role in the script is to challenge their typical male ways of viewing the world.

As two of the men approach the campfire they can be heard arguing about some obscure baseball fact. The young woman reports that she once went with a guy who was a walking encyclopedia on baseball. The following dialogue ensued:

He: *So, do you hate baseball?*

She: *No, I like baseball–I just never understood how you guys can spend so much time discussing it. I watch games, but I don't memorize who played third base for Pittsburgh in 1960.*

They (in unison): *Don Howe*

She: *That's exactly what I mean.*

He: *Then what is it that your friends talk about, out there.*

She: *Well, real life–relationships, are they working, are they not–who she's seeing, is it working.*

He: *No contest. We win!*

She: *Why?*

He: *Honey, if that were as interesting as baseball they'd have cards for it and sell it with gum.*

What a wonderful glimpse of the differences between the way men and women typically view sport!

This difference is not at all surprising to any of us who have cared enough about sport to pay attention. Clearly young men are socialized in ways that place sport in a central position in their lives, even if they themselves are not athletes. As a matter of fact, one way that the non-athletic male can gain acceptance is to become a walking encyclopedia of sports trivia. Sport is more than a pastime for most males. It is one of the most important vehicles for linking them to one another. "Sports talk" becomes the language that allows men to connect with other men.

Each day I was reminded of the centrality of sport in the life of men in urban America when I interacted with the male staff members in the high rise condo where we resided for several years. I had little in common with these men except for a shared interest in the Houston Rockets, Oilers, and Astros. This common thread bound us together, even when we were separated by barriers of race, ethnicity, age, class, and culture.

Males who fail to demonstrate a genuine interest in sport are suspect and are quickly reminded that they don't belong. Most often boys who show no interest in sport are labeled "sissies" or "fags." Young men are all too often merciless in their treatment of their age peers who do not show the necessary deference to sport. It is important in most neighborhoods to signal an affinity for what I like to call the "Trading Card Culture." Men are expected to be able to exchange sports lore and statistics as well as remain abreast of the standings of local school, college, and professional teams. While this varies from neighborhood to neighborhood, it is difficult to advance to a position of power and responsibility in a workplace or community if one does not connect with others through sport. It was not surprising to notice Texas governor, Ann Richards, at a Rockets game during her term in office. A woman has difficulty getting elected anywhere without keeping abreast of what is happening in sports in her district.

In most cases young girls growing up in America have quite different experiences, unless they are brought up in a home or neighborhood where playing with boys was the only option available. In those cases they are frequently tormented by the tension between what they enjoy doing, playing sports with the boys, and what the rest of the people in their lives are directing them to do. Even if they choose to identify with sport, it is unlikely they will ever be accepted as "one of the boys."

Our oldest daughter, who has a distinguished record of athletic achievement and has a passion for sports of all kinds, follows closely college and professional sports. She is married to a man who thoroughly appreciates her sports interests, talents, and knowledge. But, some of his male associates have difficulty including her in their "for men only" outings, even though she can hold her own with "sports talk." Inhabitants of these traditional bastions of male privilege are slow to share their turf with women. Many males are not yet ready to admit women into their exclusive groups even when they possess the knowledge and background to contribute to the life of the group. But more men today than ever before are fondly embracing women who share their interests in sport.

Some would say that sport does more than simply bond men to one another and separate them from women. Feminist critics of sport remind us that this bonding serves to preserve the power and gender advantage men enjoy in a male-led society. Therefore, sport becomes a vehicle for maintaining male dominance. While few would suggest that men consciously use sport to maintain the status quo in gender relations, the fact remains that the existence of the "Trading Card Culture" has served to isolate men from women and has allowed male networks to profoundly influence who holds political and economic power. *The City Slickers* dialogue demonstrates clearly how men have maintained the upper hand in gender relations, even in day to day interactions. They have simply discredited any perspective on sport that does not conform to their mainstream view.

What does this observation suggest regarding women and sport? Does it mean that there is a very good chance that women will be required indefinitely to remain relatively powerless outsiders because they are not being given access to the mainstream sports culture? Does it mean that women will continue to be relegated to second class citizenship until such time that the culture of sport is effectively transformed? Does it mean that women need to lead a fight to dismantle the sports establishment so that it can no longer serve as the bastion of privilege and an instrument of male domination? Or does it mean that champions for women's opportunity need to mount an aggressive effort to demand their rightful place alongside their male counterparts in the established "Trading Card Culture" so that they can become full fledged participants in sport and society?

Or is it possible that women can invite men to consider the possibility that sport could better serve everyone's interests, and therefore enrich the lives of both sexes, if men would join with women in fashioning a new vision of sport that is more inclusive by appealing to both traditional masculine and feminine values? The latter may seem attractive to those inclined to avoid a confrontational approach to social change, but it may also reflect an unsophisticated view of the realities of gender and power. First of all, most men do not see that anything is wrong, so why fix it? Is it realistic to think that men will willingly give up the privileges they enjoy from a segregated "Trading Card Culture"? Hopefully, as men and women become more sophisticated about the issues associated with gender and sport they will be better able to figure out how to make sports more inclusive and at the same time more effective in serving the public interest. I am in no way suggesting that if women were given equal access to sports and were invited to become full-fledged members of the mainstream sports culture that all would be well. Without power in the economic and political spheres women are unlikely to gain power in such cultural arenas as sport and religion.

While it is desirable for men and women to be in regular discussions about sports policies and issues, sports will only contribute fully to the public well being when some of the values that women traditionally hold are reflected in the conduct of sports programs for both men and women. At the present time, when women are admitted into the sports community, the policies and practices that govern them are too often dictated by the men's sports traditions, which Mariah Burton Nelson in *Are We Winning Yet?* describes as being guided by the military model. This model is characterized by obsessive ranking of teams and individuals according to playing statistics or earnings; authoritarian, derisive relationships between coaches and players; antagonism between opponents; and the inevitable question, "Who won?"

Burton Nelson offers what she terms the partnership model, or the female approach to sport as an alternative to the military model. This approach:
• rejects the battle, enemy mentality of the military sports model;
• rejects the notion that humiliating a player is how to "get the best out of her";
• emphasizes non-violence, discourages play when athletes are injured;
• empowers, encourages, and supports players;
• is inclusive, adjusts the rules to include players of different skill levels.[1]

This feminist critique of the Culture of Conquest makes sense to most women and to many men who are uneasy with the ways leaders of mainstream sports administer the enterprise. Burton Nelson would not be surprised to learn that many men, especially those who have taken the time to reflect on their lives as athletes, would welcome the introduction of an approach to sport that is less contentious and more friendly.

Just what is it that women bring to serious discussions about what sport ought to be, whether it is administered for men by men, for women by men, for women by men, or for men by women? Women are traditionally more relationship-oriented than men. They are concerned about how others are experiencing their connections with their parents, their friends, their lovers, their bosses, and in the sports context with their teammates and their coaches. Burton Nelson's major focus in *Are We Winning Yet?* is on relationships between athletes and their opponents, athletes and their teammates, and between coaches and athletes. She also expresses concern for the emotional and physical consequences of these relationships.

When mainstream sports are examined, it is clear that relationships and emotional consequences are subordinate to other considerations. Evidence for this conclusion is reflected in a quote by Kent Steffes, the 1992 "King of the Beach," on the men's professional volleyball tour. He is quoted in *People Magazine* as saying, "Is it important that the people on the tour like me? Not one bit. A lot of people come up to me and say they hate me."[2] It is inconceivable that a woman athlete would be inclined, in the slightest, to make such a statement. In the Culture of Conquest the outcome of the battle is the focal point of discussion. Steffes, at 24 years of age, had a track record any athlete would envy. Apparently, the bottom line for him is that he remain the "top dog." Most women and many men need more than a sense of triumph from their investment in sport. How they are able to relate to others on and off the playing field is of utmost importance to the vast majority of female athletes and to more men than one might imagine. I would suspect that behind his macho bravado Kent Steffes longs for opportunities to be supported by his colleagues on the tour.

It is difficult conceiving of Chris Evert denying the importance of relationships with her fellow tennis players. I heard her comment on a TV show about how having a child had affected her. She said,

"Hitting tennis balls doesn't teach you much about love." The implication was that giving birth to a child had indeed taught her something about love. She seems to have achieved perspective on the role of sport in the scheme of things! It's hard for me to imagine Steffes, and male athletes like him, publicly arriving at that same conclusion. Sport for many men defines their lives and keeps them firmly focused upon affirming their worth through accumulating championships and prizes, whether it be in sport or in life after sport. How they do in the tasks they undertake is what really counts for most men brought up in this society. Men need to pay closer attention to how women approach sports. Women's childhood training to become nurturing and caring people prepare them well for helping men chart new directions in sport.

Burton Nelson's partnership model is very appealing to many athletes, for it focuses on the relationship dimensions of athletic life. Clearly, when brought to the table for discussions about sports policies and practices her approach suggests directions for the conduct of the athletic enterprise. The existence of Burton Nelson's position is clearly a sign of intelligent life in sport.

I would like to build on Burton Nelson's perspective by 1) emphasizing her main theme, that is, the idea that through sport athletes can "seek together" personal satisfaction, validation and empowerment, 2) supporting the notion that athletes should receive respectful encouragement and challenge from opponents, teammates, and coaches and 3) proceeding in a manner that is both psychologically and physically safe.

However, I want to go beyond supporting these social psychological principles and introduce both aesthetic and socio-cultural considerations to the discussion. I want to call attention to, not only how experiences with sport affect athletes, but also to how they affect all of the participants in the drama of sport, individually and collectively.

Attention is shifted from relationships among athletes and between coaches and athletes to the socio-cultural dynamics of sport, that is, how social conventions influence the behavior of the entire cast and audience in athletic productions: athletes, coaches, parents, athletic administrators, cheerleaders (and other support staff), and spectators, and the institutions of which they are a part. The position taken here is that all of these actors are critical to the sports drama and must therefore become collaborators in creating uplifting, empowering athletic moments. The creation of these special moments is what sport should be all about.

In order for these special moments to be created the entire system must be in harmony, moving in the same direction. Sam Keen has concluded that, "Perhaps the greatest single advance in psychological and social theory in the last fifty years has been the emergence of systems-thinking."[3] The various participants are co-dependent, the game cannot produce uplifting athletic moments unless an atmosphere of creative cooperation is established. Rather than focusing upon the athletes, or the coaches, or the spectators, I am recommending that we look at the system itself to discover what it, as a system, requires in order for these special athletic moments to be created. Focusing upon athletes as a class, coaches as a class, spectators as a class, parents as a class, women as a class, or men as a class, does not allow us to completely understand what is happening

The materials that follow support Burton Nelson's values and observations, for she has, indeed, pointed us in the right direction. Clearly, the feminine value perspective she advances can serve as the foundation upon which a socio-cultural critique of sport can be based. Burton Nelson in her work demonstrates a clear awareness that sports are more than opportunities for individuals to grow and for relationships to develop. She observes that sport is a battleground upon which the gender wars are contested. Issues of justice, power, and dignity must be addressed if we are to clearly grasp the meaning of sport for men and women and allow it to enrich the lives of all concerned. We share a common hope for sport, that is, that it have the capacity to empower all athletes, men and women alike. I invite the reader to focus upon the system itself rather than upon any of the participants to ascertain what systemic problems are inhibiting the orchestration of uplifting athletic moments.

Many observers agree that all is not well in the world of sport, and that the current dominant perspective that guides sports policies and practices is not in the best interest of either men or women. Throughout this book I have been expressing concern about the importation into women's sports of the values, attitudes, and practices that too often do violence to the human spirit in both men's and women's gyms all across the nation. Many of these mainstream values inhibit the development of synergy, or creative cooperation, that can energize everyone and enrich the sports experience.

In women's sports there are, without a doubt, signs of intelligent life, traditions that have survived the onslaught of the legion of well meaning men and women who, as bearers of the Culture of Conquest, have joined the women's sports coaching ranks. These surviving signs of uncontaminated vitality in women's sports need to be identified, articulated, nurtured, supported, celebrated, broadcast, and exported to all levels of sport for both men and women. Many of the values that have been central to the women's sports tradition deserve to be preserved and applied in a carefully considered transformation of mainstream sport.

More specifically, what is it that women can teach men about sport? It is clear to me that men can learn much from listening, with an open mind, to what women have to say about sport. Below are sample words of caution that should be heard. The list is not meant to be all inclusive. Instead I have chosen to report several observations that suggest possibilities for mutual enrichment. It is important to understand that these are the voices of those women who have not been cooped by the male-led sports culture. My experience would lead me to believe that those women who have been drafted into the service of the military model still can find, deep in their feminine consciousness, at least a faint whisper of these cautionary notes. They have, after all, been reared as women.

1. Take sport seriously, but don't let it rule your life.

Women can teach men that sport can be a vitalizing aspect of one's life, but that when it becomes the only, or even the central, source for achieving self-affirmation, one is invariably headed for trouble. The excessive emphasis that some athletes, especially men, place upon sport requires more of it than it can deliver. If one organizes ones whole life around sports and is forced to get the majority of ones satisfaction from a single source, when something goes wrong, one is injured, is in a performance slump, or experiences the inevitable slowing down that accompanies aging, the consequences are too often catastrophic. These athletes most often find the transition to life after sport difficult, indeed. George A. Selleck in his book, *How To Play The Game of Your Life,*[4] provides an alarming report on the causalities among athletes who have failed to prepare themselves for life after sport. At this point in time women seem to be better able to keep sport in perspective.

2. Truly enjoy the intimate relationships you can establish through sports.

Women can teach men that the sports environment can become an arena for the development of rich and satisfying personal relationships, that it is not necessary to set up each teammate and each opponent as a threat to ones sense of worth. When the processes of sport are given higher priority than outcomes, as is most often the case for women, then it is possible to view ones teammates and opponents in the manner suggested by Burton Nelson's partnership model, and to use one's sports experiences to develop satisfying personal relationships. Men seldom develop true intimacy with their teammates and only rarely with their opponents.

I have been extremely impressed with the warmth and closeness of the relationships that my daughters have been able to develop with both their former college teammates and their former collegiate opponents during, and after college. In their current adult competition, which is serious volleyball and soccer, the atmosphere of their tournaments is characterized by a genuine interest in and concern for the entire community of athletes at these outings. Many of their former opponents are now their teammates and at some of the friendship tournaments rival teams exchange players and thoroughly enjoy the camaraderie of the competition. As the athletes marry and have children these new personalities, husbands and babies, are integrated into this enduring community of athletes. Men typically have specific rather than diffuse relationships with their fellow athletes (and work mates for that matter). Men could learn from women how to enrich their athletic experiences by investing in building intimacy with teammates and opponents.

3. Take fewer risks with your body.

Women can teach men to have more respect for their own and other people's bodies. Women are less willing to play hurt when such action could do permanent damage to their physical well being. Men are taught to "tough it out" and are expected to make sacrifices for Good Old State U. Some coaches would declare that women's lack of willingness to sacrifice their bodies for the good of the team is a shortcoming they need to overcome if they are to be truly successful. Clearly, all athletes play with some pain, but far too many men have been socialized into a macho mentality that puts them at risk of permanent damage to their bodies. Few of my contemporaries who participated with me in serious sport are without serious injury that continues to limit their life in some way.

4. Enjoy the grace and beauty of sport, not just the winning.

Women can teach men how to develop aesthetic sensitivities that will allow them to make sports productions artistic successes. Women value grace and agility, qualities that make pleasing complements to speed and power. When sport is at its best, it flows in ways that appeal to our aesthetic sensitivities. Women can help men enjoy those aspects of their sports experiences. If a play is "beautiful," who scores the point becomes less important, for everyone, winners or losers alike, can thoroughly enjoy the experience. Nowhere is this more evident than in tennis or volleyball competitions where opponents have long rallies where the athletes are displaying remarkably agile and graceful moves while keeping the ball in play. Everyone is enlivened by these exciting rallies, athletes and spectators alike. Opponents should celebrate together when they have shared such magnificent moments. Women seem to have a special capacity to appreciate this most important aspect of sport and get less hung up on who has been triumphant.

5. Enjoy participation, even if one is not in an elite program.

Women can teach men that sport does not have to be at the highest levels to be enjoyable. By making sport more inclusive, opportunities are provided larger numbers of athletes to be empowered by the experience. Not only will more athletes develop a passion for sport, which will allow them to be uplifted by their experiences, but also the long term interests of elite sports, whose more public and prominent productions enliven the community, will be served by preparing more people to become knowledgeable and enthusiastic patrons of sport.

6. Enjoy the ceremonial aspects of sport.

Women can teach men how to be effective participants in the ceremonies of sport. They have a sense of the importance of ritual in human affairs. Male athletes too often are self-absorbed and so excessively focused on trying to avoid defeat, that they have little patience with the details that make for good ceremony. Their impatience with ceremony is often evident as they squirm restlessly during the singing of the national anthem rather than reveling in the exhilaration of the moment. The national anthem is only one aspect of the ceremony of sport, for each athletic performance, from beginning to end, contains elements that allow it to serve the purposes of enlivening all participants.

7. Avoid violence, intimidation, and contentiousness.

Brutish conduct on the part of both athletes and coaches is tolerated, condoned, and even celebrated by many members of the men's sports community. The direct expression of anger and aggression, while discouraged by codes of sportsmanship and punishable by the rules of the game, have become central features of prime time sports. It may be because some sports promoters have concluded that it makes for good television. But whatever the rationale for allowing it to become such a central feature of men's sports it has become a annoying distraction for many athletes and spectators alike. When John Mc Enroe went into one of his tantrums his behavior disrupted the flow of the match. His opponent and the spectators who have "lost themselves" in the rhythm of the competition are awakened from that special state of enchantment that good sports create. Outbursts become rude intrusions that spoil the game for many lovers of sport.

There is much that men can teach women about sport as well. Women must not assume that simply because there are some serious problems with the way prime time sport is being conducted that there is nothing they can learn from men. Here are some lessons from the mainstream male sports culture that women can learn:

1. Accurately interpret feedback.

Too often women get their "feelings hurt" when they are offered correction about how they might better perform an athletic skill. They are often convinced that the communication means that the coach does not like them, or that the coach prefers another player whose performance they do not criticize. Women generally come to sport at an older age than men, therefore they have not developed a clear understanding of the meaning of this type of instructional feedback in the context of sport. They care very much that the coach like them as a person, that the coach appreciate every aspect of them, their skills, their heart and their soul. Men seem to be better able to under-stand that corrective feedback directed at them does not necessarily mean that the coach does not care about them. To the contrary, they have learned that an athlete should begin to worry when their coach gives up on him and does not provide feedback, either positive or negative.

2. Develop the capacity to recover quickly from a setback.

Again because men have had more experience with sport, and because men have been taught to be "tough"they typically have developed the capacity to bounce back, as they say "to suck it up," re-focus their attentions on the task at hand. Women too often remain preoccupied with their failure, their inadequacy, asking themselves questions such as whether their error will be viewed as having let down their teammates and/or their coach. This characteristic response appears to grow out of the fact that women have been socialized to keep their antenna up so that they can be responsive to all those around them. In this case a positive quality, interpersonal concern and awareness, can interfere with performance.

3. Be assertive.

In order to be competitive it is sometimes essential to assert one-self. Men are expected to be assertive in our society, whereas women are expected to be more yielding. Women can learn from men that there are times when it is OK to stand your ground. Successful ath-letic performance requires athletes to hold their ground and not be intimidated by either their opponents, their teammates, parents, or coaches.

4. Stay focused.

In athletic competition there are many occasions for distractions by the interpersonal dynamics of the situation. There are always those who are attempting to gain advantage by disrupting opponents by "talking trash." There are also times when teammates get angry at one another in the heat of competition. Women tend to be atten-tive to these communications and their performance, therefore, is sometimes negatively affected. Again we see a case where a positive characteristic, interpersonal sensitivity, becomes a negative charac-teristic when imported into the sports setting. This reality presents a challenge to those of us who are pressing for a synthesis of masculine and feminine approaches to sport.

5. Learn to play with people you do not necessarily like.

Men, over the years, have learned to chose as teammates those athletes who are the best competitors, whether or not they personally like them. The bottom line for most men is, "Can he help our team win?" Women, on the other hand, generally would be more than willing to accept a teammate with less skill who had a more pleasant personality.

If women were able to address the above issues by adopting the attitudes and learning the skills of their male counterparts, they would be in better positions to focus on creating high quality, satisfying sports performances for themselves. However, as can be seen, it is important to do so without compromising one of their greatest strengths, their interpersonal sensitivity. This tension between the tough and the tender is one of the most central issues in developing a perspective on sport that builds upon both masculine and feminine predisposition.

Women need to stay in conversation with those administering men's sports so that they can invite their male counterparts to help them adopt the attitudes and learn the skills necessary for developing fully as athletes. It is in this dialogue that women will be presented with opportunities to persuade men that they can learn something from the way they approach sport. Women will not even be able to fashion women's sports to fit their own needs and expectations without first mobilizing allies in the men's sports community. That is one of the political realities that has to be acknowledged, as discouraging as it might be to some.

That is not to say that we need to look no further than to the traditions of men's and women's sports for direction. I am calling for the search for new ways of viewing sport that will lead to significant reforms that can vitalize the enterprise in ways that are consistent with the realities of contemporary social and economic life. We must look beyond the culture of narcissism, where sport is viewed simply as a vehicle for personal fulfillment. We must attend to how sport can be used to strengthen the fabric of our social institutions and culture. Sport can do more than promote self-realization and nurture satisfying interpersonal relationships.

It was interesting to observe that as many women as men were seen on the streets of Houston in 1994 and 1995 wearing Rockets Championship T-shirts for months after the NBA finals. This development suggests that the culture of sport is performing important community-building functions where men and women are using sport to connect with one another and with their communities. Everyone benefits when men and women, boys and girls, share enthusiasm for sport. Sport, indeed, can bridge the gender gap. Men and women have a lot to teach one another about sport.

So, do women hate baseball, and other manly sports? Most of them may not collect trading cards, or follow the batting averages, shooting percentages, etc. of the stars. But some do. There are more and more women who share a passion for their home team. Since the '30s, when baseball began radio broadcasts, women have been able to enjoy witnessing this manly sport. And from time to time they have been provided opportunities to play the game in *A League of Their Own* and on Little League teams. In addition, the game of softball has been appropriated by women as a mainstay of their sports curriculum. Women are becoming more and more a part of the baseball-softball community. It seems that it will be some time before baseball-softball is significantly imprinted by the values of the Culture of Care. Some would hope that such an outcome never occurs, especially baseball traditionalists who find the continuity of the game to be comforting as everything else in their lives is being transformed. But times are changing. Nothing can be insulated from the forces that are impacting all of our institutions, including baseball. Ken Burns knows that all too well.

In my judgment one of the most interesting features of Burn's mini-series, *Baseball*, was the personal memoirs of historian Doris Kearns Goodwin. She passionately discussed the role baseball played in her relationship with her father and with her place of origin, the Bronx. Goodwin had the advantage of living near Ebbets Field and through baseball was able to develop a common ground upon which to build a relationship with her father and her neighborhood. Baseball is not as violent as other manly sports, but is a game filled with stories and drama that provide women, as well as men, with a sense of continuity and community. Many empowerment needs of women can be met simply by becoming a dedicated baseball fan. Only a small percentage of men, who invest in baseball, actually play the game.

Most importantly, the sport provides a common ground for its fans, male and female, players and spectators.

Most women who love baseball still share an interest in "real life—relationships—are they working, are they not—who she's seeing—is it working." These lively women have discovered that they too can be an integral part of the community of baseball and can use it as a common ground for connecting with other men and women and as a way to establish a sense of place and community. Rootedness becomes more and more important when people are a part of a mobile work force. New Generation women, more than any other women in history, are invading, in significant numbers, traditional male turfs, including baseball. Not only are they sharing in its "rooting," renewal, and community building benefits, but as consumers they have every right to place demands upon the institution so that it reflects their interests and values. New Generation women can leave their mark on the manly sports, including baseball, even when it is not included in the women's sports curriculum. It is important to find vehicles for expanding the common ground so that women can participate more actively in shaping the character of traditional manly sports.

Many New Generation women have a real passion for sports of all kinds. That is a very encouraging sign, not only for the institution of sport, but for relationships between men and women in all sectors of life. When women involve themselves with sport they can imprint it with Culture of Care values and use it as a tool for harmonizing family life. It is encouraging to see women involved in manly sports. With more and more mothers becoming informed and dedicated fans, serving as little league coaches, and with more and more girls playing on Little League and softball teams, baseball is being impacted by carriers of Culture of Care values. No, women do not hate baseball, especially when they are provided citizenship in the community of fans and/or players. Clearly, the more women have opportunities to play a sport, the better chance they have to imprint the game with their values.

When men and women share a common interest in a spectacle sport, such as baseball, it allows them to engage in meaningful dialogue. By sharing their interest in baseball, and any other sport for that matter, men and women can teach one another about how to get the most out of their sports experiences. Sport does not need to be a battleground in the "war between the sexes." To the contrary, the different approaches of men and women to sport can be used as sources of mutual enrichment. A common ground is essential before feminine values can be reflected in mainstream sport.

An experience that our daughters had in the early '80s, when they were in high school, demonstrated to me how women can enrich the athletic lives of men. They and a few of their gifted female volleyball players had decided to enter a coed tournament in the San Francisco Bay Area. At the time we were living in Davis, where there were no opportunities for boys to learn to play the game, so they had no young men to invite to join their team. They were undaunted by this limitation. They recruited several of the finest male athletes in their high school to play with them in the tournament. The athletes included one all-around athlete who eventually played Pac-Ten football at the University of California, a champion high jumper, a star water polo player, a basketball star, who later went on to play on the University of San Francisco team, and other gifted athletes. None of them had ever played volleyball, but were eager to learn. They had a single practice session before entering the coed event. Needless to say, this pick-up team was overwhelmed by their opponents. These gifted male athletes were humiliated by being defeated soundly by a team of undersized Asians and Americans. The boys returned to Davis with bruised egos, but a resolve to learn how to play the game. Within two years after forming a boys' team, by asking the high school girls' coach to teach them the game, they won the Northern California championship!

Several things happened as a result of that episode. The boys developed respect for the talents of the girls; they learned to enjoy a "girls game"; they established a common ground with these young women; they exposed themselves to the benefits of a non-violent game that tests a wide range of athletic talents; they learned from the girls on the team a new set of ground rules for how to soft pedal their typical aggressive style—the volleyball code prohibits the kinds of craziness one observes in the manly sports; they discovered another forum for testing their athletic talents; and they created a joint venture with male athletes from different sports. And, of course, the girls benefited too. They learned more about how boys approach sport. All in all, this experience allowed both the boys and the girls to learn new ways of approaching sport.

Everyone won, except possibly the boys' baseball, track, basketball, and water polo coaches. Some of them tried to prohibit their athletes from adding volleyball to their lives. They felt it competed with the time and energy the boys should be devoting to their sports. However, when a boy's coach demanded that one of his superstars give up volleyball, the athlete told the coach that he would rather give up the manly sport than quit volleyball. The coach reluctantly capitulated, creating an appropriate epilogue to this tale. The boys refused to be limited by the code of the manly sports community and were empowered and enlivened by their experiences with these dedicated sportswomen. And so were my daughters and their teammates. They had constructed a common ground upon which to build meaningful relationships with the boys in their lives.

Back to baseball. Not only do women like baseball, they can contribute to the enhancement of men's appreciation for the game. First of all, as New Generation women get more involved in baseball their values are more likely to find expression in the game. And that is good for men and for the game. Secondly, and without question, it is within reach of all men who love baseball to find women who are just as passionate about the game as they are. Having a partner with whom to share one's love of the game can greatly add to the renewal benefits of sport.

So, again, the question. Do women hate baseball? Surely, some do, but for generations the spirits of women have been uplifted by participation at some level in the baseball community. My mother was enriched by her regular Sunday trips to the small town ballpark with my grandfather. These outings began before World War I. Today, New Generation women, more than any other women in history, are able to participate in the orchestration of sports experiences in ways that empower participants and enliven the communities of which they are a part. This is a development that deserves to be celebrated. As men and women enjoy games of renewal together they will be better able to develop approaches to sport for the 21st century that allow all participants to be mutually enriched by their respective gender-based gifts. "His standpoint" and "her standpoint" are both essential for creating sports experiences that meet the empowerment needs of the New Generation.

CHAPTER EIGHT

Standpoints on the "Sportscape": His, Hers, and Their

As the array of TV cameras pan the playing field, the director in the control booth switches to those scenes that, in his judgment, will command viewer attention. He instructs his cameramen to zoom in on a coach on the sidelines as he angrily issues orders to his athletes, to isolate a player giving a teammate a congratulatory "high five," to secure a close-up of a group of spectators dressed in outrageous costumes celebrating their team's achievements, or he instructs his assistant to frame the scoreboard with the final seconds winding down and to be ready to call up a billboard that displays player and team statistics. There are so many developing subplots in the stadium that it is impossible for the director to bring everything into view. Even wide angle shots fail to capture all of the drama being played out. The director's choices only provide selective glimpses of a constantly changing sportscape.

Lovers of sport, as well as television directors, make decisions about which features on the playing field are worthy of their attention. What each chooses as focal points is profoundly affected by his or her training as an observer of the sports scene. The sports education we receive while growing up dictates, not only what we choose to view, but also how we view each of the scenes in the drama. Our experiences with sports on TV, in no small part, play a significant role in training us for appreciating the various dimensions of the sports experience. What and how we perceive sports scenes is also influenced by the language, images, and metaphors conveyed to us by our parents, coaches, and peers. Labels and metaphors allow us to impose some semblance of order on the universe of sport.

Men and women typically zoom in on different features of the sportscape. If there is any doubt about the differences between what men and women attend to on the playing field, I suggest comparing the eye movements of men and women at a ballgame. One will discover, in the main, that men and women are drawn to quite different scenes. By asking them what they have observed it is discovered that they generally use gender-particular language and metaphors to describe what has come into view. It is quite apparent that men and women assume different vantage points for viewing action on the field. They stand at different points as they look out over the stadium, feasting their eyes on the rich range of engaging features.

Over the past several decades, a Culture of Conquest has developed around the men's sports establishment that keeps men of all ages attending to the scoreboard, stat sheets, traditional rivalries, superstars, home team loyalties, flamboyant coaches, and zealous spectators. These various features of the sportscape make for entertaining television and feed American men's insatiable appetites for sports drama of all kinds. This pervasive culture, which, at least in part, is the creation of a multi-billion dollar marketing effort by the sports industry, is enthusiastically supported by a loyal corps of writers, broadcasters, and advertisers. These messengers of mainstream sports traditions are members of a massive marketing team that is waging a vigorous campaign to increase demand for all manner of sports properties: teams, superstars, coaches, publications, and especially sporting goods.

While women constitute a significant proportion of consumers of sports products and services, they have been slow to adopt the language, metaphors, and values of the mainstream sports culture. Also their upbringing has made it difficult for them to keep focused on the same features of the playing field as are the men, for most women in their early years have been taught the language and values of the Culture of Care. This culture embraces conventional conceptions of feminine nurturing. The angel is the symbol for the Culture of Care, whereas the warrior represents the Culture of Conquest. Typically, women view sport from a distinctive feminine standpoint. Their perspective keeps them focused upon processes rather than upon outcomes; upon personal relationships with teammates, friends, and family; upon how spectators are reacting to one another and to the game; upon the needs of those less fortunate or gifted; upon the intrinsic satisfactions that can be derived from the sports activity itself; upon remaining fit; upon helping one's "sisters" achieve parity in sports; upon gaining public acceptance of sports for women; and upon growing personally through the sports activity.

However, the increasing numbers of young women who are currently progressing through the women's sports system, are typically educated by men and women who promote the values of mainstream sports. These values are deeply rooted in success-oriented masculine traditions. Meanwhile, the popular media and most other people in the lives of young women continue to impress upon them the desirability of embracing traditional feminine values. These are confusing times to be a young woman in America, especially if she chooses to enter a non-traditional arena like sport. While women have now been given permission to leave the bleachers for the playing field, most continue to view sports from a traditional feminine standpoint, no longer from the perspective of the stands, but from a point on the sportscape profoundly influenced by their upbringing as women.

Even with the most competitive of women athletes, their socialization into the Culture of Care continues to reveal itself in their attitudes toward sport. In an interview with Billy Jean King, one of tennis' most intense competitors, she exposes a fundamental difference between masculine and feminine perspectives on sport as she comments about the benefits of selecting women as coaches:

From the time we are born we're taught to think "we" instead of "I." We're taught to look, listen, and worry about others. That makes us very nurturing. Men could do this too, but often they just want to take care of their own egos.[1]

While King's statement might be interpreted as "male bashing" by some, it does seem to point to a significant difference between how men and women approach sport. Billy Jean King, as completely as she bought into the values of mainstream sports, still reveals the effects of being reared a woman. Probably, when she was growing up, no one was more of a tomboy. Yet, in spite of all the male influences in her life and all those years of high profile competition, the Culture of Care continues to shape her perceptions of the sports experience. In my judgment, this is good news. It indicates that traditional feminine qualities are too robust to be destroyed, even by years and years of immersion in a highly competitive professional sports environment. Competition does not necessarily have to do violence to ones concern for the welfare of others. It makes me feel that, indeed, it is possible to fashion sports policies and practices that keep this feminine predisposition alive as women throw themselves into competitive sports.

Since the Culture of Conquest guides mainstream sports, it seems appropriate to position it as the sports thesis of our day with the Culture of Care, a faint antithesis. The presence of the Culture of Care, even though it has a low profile in the world of sport, is still able to produce a creative tension, since so many women in and out of sports (including mothers of athletes) are intuitively comfortable with its values.

Therefore, one assumption I am making is that most women athletes, because of their early socialization as women, would find attractive those sports programs that are closely allied with the values of the Culture of Care. But I am also assuming that many managers of men's and women's programs firmly believe that a woman's socialization into the Culture of Care is one of the reasons why she has such a difficult time developing "mental toughness," a characteristic believed by so many as critical to the success of athletes (and they would add, critical to success in the rough and tumble "real world" beyond sports). These beliefs are in the majority at this point in time. One of the goals of many mainstream sports leaders is to reeducate women athletes in traditional masculine norms and values so that they can adapt to the requirements of rigorous competition. The position taken here is that sport for both men and women would be more empowering and enlivening if all athletes were urged to give expression to their feminine as well as their masculine side. This is not happening to any great extent at the moment.

For the good of sport and the welfare of current and future athletes it seems important for mainstream sports to be challenged. Fortunately, it is being challenged every day by a variety of voices which express discomfort with the direction sport is taking, but these voices are most often isolated, not organized, and hence too quickly ignored or dismissed. But as I listen to both men and women evaluate mainstream sports I hear a consistent expression of concern. These critics seem to be searching for a new vision of sport, one that reflects the feminine voice that speaks clearly to nearly all women and more faintly to most men.

There is concern among New Generation men and women that sport is losing its capacity to be uplifting to both participants and spectators. Lasch articulates that point of view:

The mania for winning has encouraged an exaggerated emphasis on the competitive side of sport, to the exclusion of the more modest but more satisfying experiences of cooperation and competence. The cult of victory, proclaimed by such football coaches as Vince Lombardi and George Allen, has made savages of players and rabid chauvinists of their followers. The violence and partisanship of modern sports lead some critics to insist that athletics impart militaristic values to the young, irrationally inculcate local and national pride in the spectator, and serve as one of the strongest bastions of male chauvinism.[2]

Lasch's description of the mainstream "cult of victory" reflects the sentiments of many lovers of sport. What he describes is a relatively recent development. More and more people are finding that sport fails to satisfy their fundamental needs for empowerment, enlivenment, enchantment, and renewal.

If we are to construct an alternative to the Culture of Conquest that reflects the values that New Generation men and women are bringing onto the playing field, it will be necessary to 1) clarify the nature of the masculine values that currently govern sport, 2) allow for the expression of those feminine voices that are challenging mainstream sports policies and practices, 3) search for a common ground upon which the masculine and feminine can meet, and 4) effect a synthesis of the old and the new, consistent with basic human needs, the social requirements of our times, and gender-just principles of social responsibility.

Sport can be one of the most fruitful arenas in which to work on the task of clarifying norms that govern how men and women live their lives together. As one addresses the fundamental issues surrounding how women ought to relate to sport, it becomes necessary to pay careful attention to all of the difficult challenges associated with fashioning a sex role for oneself, whether one is male or female, young or old. When debating men's and women's sports policies it is difficult to sweep any of the fundamental issues of gender relations under the rug. Not only are we able to come to a better understanding of men's and women's sports in these discussions, but by addressing these issues we are also forced to consider the goals we hold for men and women in other sectors of life as well.

Below, I have described three different cultural standpoints that can be used to view the sports experience. These are ideal types put forward to identify and clarify issues of sports policy and practice. No one person takes a consistent stance across the various issues, for there are men who are comfortable with many of "her standpoints" and women who are comfortable with many of "his standpoints." This framework has been advanced in order to contrast significantly different positions taken by a majority of men and women in relation to sports issues. These standpoints grow out of the distinctive ways men and women are taught to live their lives. I use the term standpoint to indicate where the person stands in relation to other points on the sportscape to which he is attracted or repelled. A sportscape includes all those images of which one can be conscious while having, or reflecting upon, a sports experience. The sportscape is composed of sports-related features of an individual's life space or psychological environment that have attracting or repelling qualities.

"His standpoint" (the thesis) reflects the position of the mainstream sports culture, the Culture of Conquest. "Her standpoint" (the antithesis) reflects the position of an authentic feminine perspective, the Culture of Care, uncontaminated by traditional masculine values. And "Their standpoint" (the synthesis) suggests a shared, New Generation position that I would expect to result from a successful challenge to the mainstream sports culture by a renewed, re-energized feminine perspective on sport. This synthesis is the common ground upon which men and women stand after they have come to appreciate the sportscape from the vantage point of the Other. I am choosing to refer to this synthesis as the Culture of Counterpoint.

While a synthesis is likely to occur as "her standpoint" gains prominence, the outcomes of the tension between the masculine and feminine standpoints are not always going to be found satisfactory by everyone. Each new perspective that grows out of the dialectical process must be put to test, using ones ethical principles to judge whether the new position makes sense in relation to the social requirements of the time and the empowerment needs of those involved. It is important to understand that "their standpoint," deriving from the Culture of Counterpoint, may not always seem to be the most relevant and growth enhancing. However, "their standpoint" does seem to be the most likely position to emerge as a result of competition between masculine and feminine perspectives. What I am asserting is that a synthesis is a high probability outcome of a vigorous challenge of mainstream sports by carriers of feminine values, and that in many cases a New Generation synthesis represents an option that will allow for the expression, through sport, of both masculine and feminine predisposition. But I am also observing that each synthesis must be challenged and tested as it emerges as the new thesis to determine whether it is in the best interest of men, women, and the communities of which they are a part. One can expect that today's common ground will find itself under attack from future generations. Undoubtedly tomorrow's leaders will face new social requirements that call for the reform of sports policies and practices. However, while social requirements change over time, the existential or empowerment needs of men and women remain the same as do universal principles of equality, justice, and dignity. Balancing social requirements, personal needs, and principles of interpersonal responsibility is a perennial challenge.

The most effective way to test the usefulness of the "his, hers, and theirs" analytic framework is to examine some of the questions that need to be addressed when developing sports policies and practices. Below I am suggesting how this debate might be played out if mainstream sport, "his standpoint," is challenged by a strong feminine voice, "her standpoint." "Their standpoint" is an outcome I would expect to find being articulated with increasing frequency as those endowed with a New Generation consciousness secure high profile platforms for sharing their vision.

What is the coach's role?

His standpoint: Coaches should be competent in developing their athletes' talents, and in judging fairly their ability to contribute to the team.

Her standpoint: Coaches should have the ability to demonstrate positive regard for all their athletes, and show concern for them as total-human beings.

Their standpoint: Coaches should be competent, fair, and be able to show genuine respect for their athletes, encouraging them to produce athletic moments that empower and enliven all concerned.

Traditional beliefs about how coaches ought to carry out their roles have been guided by a preoccupation with the scoreboard. Does the coach get results, that is, do his teams win? The methods he uses to accomplish his objectives are generally of less concern than the results. If he has to threaten, intimidate, shake, hit, punish, or demean his athletes to win, so be it, goes the conventional wisdom. As long as the coach is fair and plays within the "rules," that's all that really counts. Vince Lombardi is reputed to have said "I treat all my athletes the same, like dirt." One of football's highest awards has been named after Lombardi, demonstrating the Culture of Conquest's respect for the hard-nosed approach to sport that he represents. George Raveling, former men's basketball coach at the University of Southern California, reveals the extent to which he feels the Lombardi mentality pervades the coaching community when he says in a *New York Times* article, in the wake of the firing of a successful coach for verbally abusing athletes, "If you fired every coach who swore or yelled, unemployment in this country jumps 10%." I'm sure many of his colleagues would join him in his implied conclusion, "Everybody does it, so what's the big deal?" Nearly the entire coaching and sports writing community expressed outrage in 1993 when Lou Campanelli was fired at California for verbally abusing his athletes.

Duke's Mike Krzyzewski, one of men's basketball's most highly respected coaches and known for his relatively restrained approach to motivating athletes, made it clear that serious sports competition is a "man's game" when he reportedly told his team (when they were down one point at half time to Michigan in 1993) that they were "playing like weak sissies." In mainstream sports, the coach, until recently, has been given carte blanche to do and say whatever it takes to get the win, even if it means demeaning young men by putting down the abilities of women. Since Coach K's team went on to win the game, his magical sexist language has now become, in all probability, a part of his motivational arsenal. Frustration and anger seem to be the "creative" inspiration for these ritualistic demeaning incantations.

Nowhere was there better evidence of this type of anger-inspired verbal abuse than in a news report describing the conduct of coach John Chaney of Temple University during a critical point in their quarter final game against Michigan in the 1993 NCAA championships. When he was assessed with a technical foul for using profanity with the referee, he retorted that he was not using profanity with the referee, but instead was addressing one of his players, forcefully inviting him to retaliate against the rough treatment he was receiving from a Michigan player. He was overheard saying "If (the referee) won't call it, put (the opposing player) on the floor." Chaney clearly understood it was against the rules to swear at a referee, but apparently he believed it was OK to swear at one of his athletes and to instruct him to take violent action against an opponent. The most telling aspect about this incident is that there was no public reaction by either Chaney's peers or by the press to this outburst of uncontrolled anger. This "no call" suggests that his conduct is considered by the mainstream sports culture as being within acceptable boundaries. Most participants in the Culture of Conquest not only tolerate these kinds of assaults on the dignity of athletes, but also articulate grave concern about those New Generation athletes who increasingly are challenging abusive coaching tactics.

Not only coaches but sports writers and hard core fans are expressing alarm about the increasing incidence of high profile challenges to traditional command and control approaches to handling athletes. They see no reason to tamper with a good thing. However, New Generation athletes, the sons and daughters of the baby boomers who challenged established political and educational authority during the Viet Nam War, are often less willing to accept, without question, the tough and sometimes abusive approaches that have been tolerated, even venerated, in past eras.

Also as more women are entering into serious sports training some widely employed coaching strategies are being re-evaluated. Approaches that fathers and mothers find tolerable with their sons they find difficult to accept when applied to their daughters. However, there has been a trend for coaches of women to emulate the successful coaches of men, as coaches of women have struggled to gain acceptance by their colleagues and their superiors. In spite of this pressure to conform, women have brought to the world of sport values that challenge typical drill sergeant approaches to sports leadership. While it would be an exaggeration to conclude that women are making many in-roads in transforming the ways men typically approach coaching, it seems fair to say that the presence of girls and women in the gym and on the playing field is provoking at least some re-evaluation of traditional coaching practices. A challenge to the typical masculine approach to coaching is clearly articulated by Dr. Donna Lopiano, former University of Texas Women's athletic director and currently president of the Women's Sports Foundation.

As an athletic director for 17 years, I've had the opportunity to hire many coaches. And the best coaches are a combination of the strength that we see of men in our society and the sensitivity of women. I truly believe the best coaches have been women. There have been few men who have had that sensitivity. When you combine the two, the feminine quality is just wonderful in terms of mentally dealing with an athlete and being sensitive and picking up things right up front. [3]

The masculine standpoint on the role of the coach is still dictated by a primary focus on outcomes and fairness, while the feminine standpoint is strongly affected by concern for the welfare of the participants. The masculine approach is founded upon the belief that individuals are naturally passive or "lazy" as many male coaches are fond of saying. Many women, on the other hand, tend to be more comfortable with a theory of motivation that assumes that individuals are basically energetic and truly want to participate with enthusiasm, but have been discouraged by experiencing all too frequent putdowns. This difference in outlook, in all probability, derives from the experiences of women as they have attempted to live their lives fully, only to be told that "little girls don't do that." Furthermore, mothers have opportunities to see the spontaneous zest for life that children possess before they are exposed to the social constraints that all too often cause children to resist efforts to get them to do what adults want them to do. Fathers most frequently are denied by circumstances and cultural expectations regular opportunities to be reminded of the natural inclinations of their children.

A synthesis of the masculine and feminine positions is emerging in the rhetoric of those brave souls, primarily on the women's side, who have been pioneering approaches to coaching that combine elements of both the masculine and feminine. Lopiano, as a women's sports activist, has done more than simply articulate a New Generation position. She, in fact, put into place, during her 17-year tenure at Texas, policies and practices that were designed to integrate the best of both the masculine and feminine traditions. An examination of the records of achievement of her Texas teams will attest to the fact that it was not necessary to abandon the ambition of producing winners while employing more athlete-centered approaches to coaching, for her teams distinguished themselves by earning numerous national titles. I'm sure, however, that she would be the first to admit that not all of her coaches, even under her strong leadership, were able to infuse their programs with the kinds of sensitivity she celebrates. But there are glimpses here and there that suggest that it is, indeed, possible to effect a synthesis of masculine and feminine approaches without abandoning ambitions of producing winning teams.

Further evidence that a New Generation standpoint is emerging can be found in the bold actions that have been taken by several athletic directors in recent years to fire prominent coaches who employ abusive command and control approaches. While the response of the coaching community and most sports writers reflect that the overwhelming majority of them are compelled to defend the old ways, there are some modest signs that "her standpoint" is gaining greater currency among those responsible for monitoring athletic programs. It is also clear that the new breed of athletes often find the old ways outrageous, archaic and out of phase with what is happening in other sectors of their lives. Those who protest are often children of parents who have adopted a more tender pattern of child rearing, a development that old guard coaches are quick to criticize. Digger Phelps, the former Notre Dame basketball coach, responding to the rash of challenges by athletes to coaching authority, bitterly speaks out:

These kids are getting spoiled earlier and earlier. Now every kid wants to be Shaquille O'Neal. It starts in the eighth grade, and by the time they're in high school they're monsters.[4]

An alternative to the excesses to which some athletes are responding has been imported from the women's side. This approach is based upon the assumption that athletes deserve to be treated with dignity and respect. It is beginning to find support throughout the community of athletes and coaches and among program monitors: faculty members, college presidents, involved parents and those sports lovers who have discovered sources of joy in sport that go beyond simply winning. While I do not expect to see a radical transformation in coaching practices in the near future, it does seem that there is no turning back. Coaches of New Generation athletes will have to re-evaluate coaching traditions and adapt them to the realities of modern day life. In my judgment the adaptations will be influenced to a great extent by traditional nurturing feminine values which support the empowerment of all those involved in the athletic enterprise.

What is the parent's role?

His standpoint: Fathers should serve as athletic models for their children, while mothers should be there to salve their children's "wounds" when they experience setbacks.

Her standpoint: Mothers should serve as athletic models for their children while fathers should support and encourage equally their sons and daughters in their athletic careers.

Their standpoint: Fathers and mothers should both be available for mentoring and supporting roles.

Fathers of past generations of athletes have been the primary carriers of the mainstream culture of sport to both their sons and daughters. Mothers have been expected to be there to cheer on their children, but are expected to have no expertise in the techniques of sport. Times are changing. The new generation of mothers of young athletes is populated with more and more women who have had at least some direct experience with sport. If they have not been competitive athletes, they have become informed students of prime time sports by sharing these experiences with the men in their lives, their fathers, husbands and even their sons. It is not uncommon to find mothers and sons attending professional and college sports events together, where they both make an effort to educate one another about what is happening on the playing field. More wives are being included in their husband's conversations about mainstream sports. This is not to say that we have witnessed a major transformation on this score, for, in the main, men have still not granted their spouses full citizenship in their exclusive world of sports.

In addition to the greater accessibility of sport to women through the media, the fact that there are so many single mothers who have the responsibility of rearing their children alone makes it essential that they inform themselves about athletics so that their children are not short changed in a society that places so much emphasis upon sports. Moms are coaching Little League teams upon which both their sons and daughters are playing. Most mothers do not want their children to be disadvantaged by being denied the benefits of a father in the house.

The presence of women in the coaching boxes and at practices cannot help but have several effects. First, women will become more expert on sports issues. Secondly, their interest in sport will increase. And thirdly, the presence of women on the playing fields, who have been socialized in the Culture of Care, will surely infuse those sports activities with feminine values. Here we have a case where the realities of the New Generation family are provoking a significant invasion of a traditional male turf, the playing field. The long term result will have to be a synthesis of his and her standpoints. The Culture of Counterpoint is within sight, if oh so far in the distance.

How should athletes relate to sports tasks (passing, shooting, kicking, stroking, etc.)?

His standpoint: Tasks are to be mastered and controlled.

Her standpoint: Tasks are to be savored and experienced.

Their standpoint: Tasks are to be mastered and savored as athletes become totally immersed in these tasks for their own enjoyment.

Because the outcomes of sport are considered so important to males, it becomes essential that they gain control over basic sports skills so that they become masters of their destinies. For men, sport is, indeed, a most serious enterprise. On the other hand, for women, sport is not generally as central to their identities, so sports skills can be approached in a quite different way. A women can still maintain her feminine identity if she fails at sport. As a matter of fact, in some cases to fail actually serves to confirm a women's femininity. Not so with men. Failure at sport is very often viewed as a sign that they are "less than a man."

The different ways men and women approach sport affect what they get out of their experiences. With men being so focused upon the outcomes of sport, they view it as a way for them to test their skills in competitive situations. In this way they are able to confirm that they are worthy of membership in the Culture of Conquest. Women, on the other hand, while also enjoying the test, more often are concerned with the processes of participation. Is sport providing them with opportunities to interact with individuals they enjoy? Does it feel good to work out? Is the execution of skills beautiful to witness? These are the kinds of questions women are likely to ask themselves in deciding whether to invest in a sports activity. Furthermore, women are much more likely to participate in sport for its own sake, since achievement in sport is not instrumental to becoming a woman.

There is no doubt in my mind but that when these two quite different orientations are combined in creative ways opportunities for growth and enjoyment are significantly enhanced. As long as the roles of women and men remain as they have been for so long, the prospects for achieving a synthesis of these two approaches seem slim, indeed. However, if the trends toward a redefinition of sex roles continues, where it becomes less important for men to use sport as a primary means of affirming their masculinity and where it becomes more attractive for women to use sport as a context in which to develop new dimensions of themselves, then we can expect to discover more evidence of a synthesis of the two standpoints in sports policies and practices.

How should athletes relate to opponents?

His standpoint: Opponents are the enemy to be conquered.

Her standpoint: Opponents are members of ones extended sports family.

Their standpoint: Opponents are collaborators in a performance, agreeing to certain rules, etc.

Vince Lombardi, a legendary spokesman for "his" sports tradition, has articulated a psychology of motivation that seems to have achieved widespread support, especially among men's team sports:

All week long there builds up in you a competitive animosity toward that other man, that counterpart across the field. All week long he is the symbol, the epitome of what you must defeat... To play this game, you must have that fire in you, and nothing stokes that fire like hate.[5]

The case of John Chaney cited earlier, where during a moment of frustration with the referees, he instructed his player to put his Michigan opponent "on the floor," indicates that the Lombardian spirit is still alive and well. For many men, opponents are "symbols," not partners, in staging a test of one's skills. It is probable, however, that the Lombardian position is viewed by many of today's men and women as an extreme that is no longer in sync with the values and realities of the '90s. Could it be that the emergence of tenderness in so many sectors of contemporary life is beginning to reveal itself in the ways men are approaching their opponents in sport? If it is true that men are becoming more tender, it is likely that they are ambivalent over what had been considered, until recently, a widely accepted standard for viewing opponents. This ambivalence can be taken as evidence we are entering an age of reevaluation of some of the most hallowed traditions in men's sports.

Most women have never really bought into an adversarial view of opponents. They have been much more likely to work hard to make sure that they did not do anything in their relationship with an opponent that would compromise the possibilities for a cordial, if not friendly, relationship. Most men have not thought that way. In life outside of sport men have been socialized to consider all other men as competitors for the limited rewards that exist out there in "real life." They have been taught to take care not to reveal to potential competitors their innermost feelings or any of their personal weaknesses. Women, while deriving so much satisfaction from the processes of sports competition, have been able to approach their opponents quite differently.

This readiness to develop cordial relationships with opponents is revealed to me in the case of our daughters' enthusiasm for joining together with former collegiate opponents in forming an adult team to compete in local, regional, and national tournaments. It is not the fact that they have joined together to compete that impresses me, for men do that as well, but it is the ease with which they and their colleagues were able to establish intimate relationships that signaled that they had not built up animosity over several years of competing against one another in collegiate competition. Men will play with former opponents if they think it will help them win, but they are most often reluctant to develop close personal relationships with them. However, times are changing. A synthesis between "her standpoint" and "his standpoint" appears to be in the wind.

How should athletes relate to teammates?

His standpoint: Teammates are either facilitators of achievement and/or competitors for a position on the team.

Her standpoint: Teammates are friends, but also potential competitors for male acceptance.

Their standpoint: Teammates are partners who complement one another's interests and talents.

In sports it has always been important to be a team player. What that has come to mean to men and women at different times in the history of American sport gives us a clue as to where we have been, where we are, and where we are going. In the past, teammates were school chums who got together to have some fun. Today, for men, teammates have come to be thought of as competitors for playing time and recognition, but also as essential for accomplishing shared goals, that is, achieving victory and all of the accolades and rewards that go with success. But how might the male standpoint be transformed if feminine values were to assume greater prominence? Many women seem to be at least as concerned with the personal qualities their teammates possess as they are with the sports skills they display.

Through their experiences with pick-up games men learn that it does not matter whether teammates are likable as long as they can help you win. I do not see that changing radically over the next decades, since that pick-up pattern of operation is similar to how so many business and government organizations currently operate. It is not unusual in today's world for workers routinely to move from one problem solving group to another to meet the needs of companies that are adjusting to a changing marketplace. It has recently been projected that the number of temporary contract workers will increase from 25% to 35% of the work force by the turn of the century. That compares with just 20% a decade ago. In an information age that requires so much specialized knowledge to solve problems in a rapidly changing world it seems likely that this pattern of operation will continue to prevail for the foreseeable future. Furthermore, as women occupy more and more of these problem solving roles, I do anticipate that they will require their groups, even if they are temporary, to supply more opportunities for emotional nourishment. In this sense, one could anticipate that the inclusion of women in sports will cause traditional male conceptions of team membership to be nudged in the direction of the feminine model. These team climates might then become more empowering and enlivening for all concerned, athletes, coaches, and spectators alike. Over the long run, a compromise position between simply being a facilitator and being a friend is likely to come into being, where teammates are viewed as partners who complement one another's interests and talents, but at the same time serve as sources of emotional support for one another.

How should athletes relate to spectators?

His standpoint: Spectators should be used to help conquer an opponent.

Her standpoint: Spectators should be entertained and treated like family.

Their standpoint: Spectators should be brought into the ceremony of sport so that they too can be enlivened and renewed by the experience.

A current fashion on the playing field is for athletes to turn to the crowd to whip them into a frenzy in support of the home team. In my day, such conduct would have been considered bad form. The athlete would have been labeled a "showboat" and found himself on the bench until he had learned his lesson. (My coaches did not even allow me to dunk during game situations for fear it would brand me as a "hot dog.") Times have indeed changed. A whole different attitude has developed around prime time sports. Anything that makes a sporting event into more of a spectacle is prized by everyone. Men have come to understand that spectators are a part of the show and that they need to use the crowd to help them in any way possible. In football it's a deafening cheer. In basketball it is the vigorous waving of arms behind the basket when an opponent is shooting a foul shot. The crowd is the home team's friend and is considered something to be used in the service of winning. Again men have a very instrumental attitude toward crowds as they do toward nearly everything on the sportscape.

Women, on the other hand, in most settings are accustomed to playing before crowds made up primarily of player families and close friends. There is quite a different relationship between the athlete and the crowd in this setting. For women, sports events are not a spectacle that they are attempting to orchestrate, but instead a competitive, non-contentious environment where they can feel supported in their efforts to put forth their best effort. Seldom do crowds for women's sports get out of control, and seldom do women athletes goad the crowd to action.

What is suggested by these two quite different patterns of relationship to spectators? In this case, I would predict that the approach used by men is establishing the direction for a new synthesis. Without question, there is no turning back the clock on sports in a TV age. Sports for both men and women will undoubtedly become more and more of a spectacle as they are show-cased on television. This need not do serious violence to the spirit of the games if it does not take a mean and violent turn, which it has been known to do from time to time.

As women become a greater part of the viewing public, both at home and in the bleachers, their inclination to be concerned about the impact of crowd participation on the feelings of the performers will prevent them from being a party to mean-spirited actions. When I go to sporting events of all types, it is nearly always men who are doing the booing and verbal intimidating from the stands. As women become more involved and sophisticated in sports will we see them displaying an insensitivity to the athletes on the field? I think not, at least to any great extent. Instead I would predict that as time goes on we will find crowds more active than ever, but if women are successful in bringing their values into the stadium, the crowds will be every bit as joyful, but also will show the performers greater consideration and respect. When sport becomes more of a ceremony for the empowerment of athletes and the renewal of communities, then it will take on more of the qualities of sacred celebrations of human possibilities. In these celebrations the welfare of everyone involved in the sports enterprise, the athletes, coaches, parents, and spectators will be taken into account. In my judgment, such a synthesis of his and her standpoints is clearly within reach.

To underscore the special relationship between a performer and spectators I am sharing a report I filed after making a trip to the Compact Center in Houston to witness one of the world's greatest prima donnas.

On a cold night in February, as my wife and I pulled our car into our usual parking space at the Compact Center, the home of the Houston Rockets, we were filled with anticipation for the treat that was in store for us inside the arena. We would be witness to a performance by one of the world's greatest. As we walked with the crowd through the underground garage to the arena entrance there was a sense of excitement in the air. This was going to be a very special evening, indeed, two hours of sheer joy. There is always the possibility that the superstar, who drew a near record crowd to the Compact Center, will not perform up to his usual level, but the "Big Guy" has always been a consistent performer whether playing in Houston or at any of the other stops throughout the country. He is a big draw every-

where. His virtuosity and consistency are legendary and he has even been a big attraction when on tour in Europe. There is something magical about his presence that commands everyone's full attention. In part I'm sure it is because of his size, but also his graceful fluid movements and his strong masculine qualities cause men and women alike to flock to watch him perform. He always captures the spectators with his exuberance and joy. National TV exposure, of course, has not hurt his popularity. And not too long ago when he appeared at an all-star event with other superstars, attendance broke all time records. He possesses an infectious charm as well as tremendous virtuosity. Even though he may have already reached his peak as a performer, he is older than most of his competitors, no one that night allowed themselves to even imagine that he might be "over the hill." Fans never want their heroes to fade from the scene and are forgiving if a performance is slightly below their best. As much as basketball fans hated to lose Michael Jordan to retirement at his peak, they were pleased not to have to witness the decline of the greatest player to ever play the game. That special night at the Compact Center no one worried that the superstar would fail to deliver. They had paid a record $736,000 for the privilege of being in the crowd. Top entertainment is not cheap these days.

As we approached the entrance we noticed that it was taking longer than usual to enter the arena. When we got to the door the explanation for the delay became apparent. There were far more women going through the turnstiles than usual, and since all women have to open their purses for inspection it took longer to get the spectators into the arena. As we passed through the gate we were greeted by an attendant who issued us a bright full-color poster that featured the superstar in various poses. It was sponsored by a national retailer with whom the superstar has been associated for some time. The poster was beautifully done and unlike so many other handouts that my wife and I have received at Rockets games this was a work of art that we brought home to keep as a momento for our grandchildren.

Usually when we walk down the corridor on our way to our seats we are greeted by two fisted beer drinkers stocking up before heading for their seats. That night the concession stands were doing a brisk business, but instead of beer there were many more fans standing around in the hallways sipping mixed drinks. Also you could tell this was a special night at the Compact Center since so many men were outfitted in suits and ties. Ticket prices are so high now that events have to depend upon corporate block sales, which means that corporate executives are over represented in the crowd. While there are always a lot of women "dressed to kill" at the Compact Center, that night nearly every woman had on her best. Clearly they were expecting something special.

As we made our way to the upper deck I noted that there were more older people struggling up the steep stairways than usual. My guess is that the average age of the spectators that evening was at least 20 year older than the normal Rockets crowd. That made them no less enthusiastic about what was to come.

When the "Big Guy" made his grand entrance, the crowd acknowledged his presence with the type of standing ovation he has grown accustomed since he has been on top. He waved to the crowd like the real pro he is, communicating his appreciation for their respect and recognition.

And quite a show did he put on. Each time, he upstaged all of the other performers. While anywhere else the virtuosity of the "others" would rate rave reviews, when the "Big Guy" is in their midst they understand that everyone has come to watch him perform. He is, of course, Luciano Pavoratti.

Later that week we attended a Rockets game that featured Hakeem Olajuwon in the pursuit of the NBA crown, and MVP recognition. It was an interesting contrast between the performer-crowd relationship. In both cases there was virtuosity, style, charm, and exuberance to spare. Both evenings the crowd was uplifted by the performances of the superstars. And during both performances there was a love affair between the crowd and the performer. At the ballgame one would expect that "His Standpoint" would prevail. It should be the "conquest" that would bring Olajuwon the attention. The competition is, of course, a factor that distinguishes a game from a concert. But I have come to understand that there were some common features to these two events that suggest that good sports and good music satisfy some of the same basic human cravings. The aesthetic dimensions of watching an accomplished athlete perform superhuman feats are not that much different than listening to a world class tenor. We are all uplifted by experiences of awe. Both Olajuwon and Pavoratti are indeed awesome in so many different ways. I saw evidence of "Their standpoint" at both performances. Spectators were brought into the ceremonies of sport and music so that they could be enlivened and renewed by the experience. The events required a different type of expertise in order to enjoy them, but there is little doubt that both audiences could have been renewed by the other performance, without the benefit of schooling. The performances were both special and hence uplifting.

At these two Compact Center events all spectators were winners because they entered the sanctuary of the arena, where they left the trials and tribulations of their daily lives at the door. The performances in this versatile building renewed the spirits of both audiences. Feminine aesthetic standards of evaluating a performance can be applied in both cases. They were, indeed, beautiful performances and the spectators were without a doubt entertained and treated like a part of the superstar's family. At the same time, there was no doubt that the stars were "real men." They are obsessive achievers, dedicated to being the best in their respective fields. The values of the Culture of Counterpoint were evident in the relationship between the performers and their witnesses, revealing the presence of both masculine and feminine qualities.

What is the role of the media?

His standpoint: The media should be used to promote athletes, the team, the coach, and the organization.

Her standpoint: The media should be educated about women's sports and women's sports issues so that they will view them as newsworthy.

Their standpoint: The media should be recruited as allies in the production of quality sports experiences.

Nothing in the history of American sport has transformed the activity any more than television, which in turn has provoked an insatiable appetite for interminable reports and debates in the print media. The media are the chroniclers and statisticians for the predominantly male "Trading Card Culture." Likewise, no other group has had such an influence over the course of sport. The media, not only report what has occurred, but generously offer their commentary and criticism. And on slow news days it appears that they are really stretching to fill their space, sometimes even fabricating conflict to create drama.

They are, without a question, a critical component of the sports entertainment industry.

More than a few coaches and athletic directors have been replaced by the public furor initiated, reflected, and amplified by sports writers. Sports commentators also have had a significant effect upon the careers of untold numbers of athletes. When a prominent sports writer challenges a coach about the use of his athletes or his game strategy, it seldom escapes notice by the coach. There is no doubt that sports writers are major architects of the sportscape, whether or not we feel they have the credentials to assume that role.

What values do sportswriters typically bring to their reporting and commentating? More often than not they speak from "his standpoint." While only a few sports writers have had distinguished careers as athletes, most broadcast media commentators have their roots on the playing field of men's sports. In nearly all cases, even when commentators are women, members of the media enthusiastically embrace the values of the Culture of Conquest. Occasionally an iconoclast will appear on the scene, but in the main they all march to "his" drummer.

The messengers of the mainstream sports culture are the conservators of the language of the Culture of Conquest. When they describe sports events they remind us of how deeply their culture is rooted in military traditions. It is common to read reports that proclaim: "The Rockets chewed up the Denver Nuggets in the second half and left the mile high gang a bloody mess, inflicting a 107-96 wound on the Nuggets."[6] "His standpoint" is clearly articulated in the media each and every day.

His and her standpoints on the role of the media are similar in that they both seek to have sports accurately reported and effectively promoted by the masters of the media. Women in sports are faced with an additional challenge. The media typically report those events and stories they believe will be of interest to their readers or viewers. The modest coverage of women's sports by the media is justified by the generally accepted conclusion that there is not enough interest in it to warrant the time and space. There is no doubt that the writers and sportscasters are right in claiming that there is little general public interest in reports of women's sports. However, until there is more publicity for women's sports, little interest is likely to grow. But is it the responsibility of the commercial press to promote special interest groups, even in the service of achieving gender equity? Most of those in the media business say no. And certainly there are no laws on the books that require equal reporting. Furthermore, I have heard few commentators calling for that type of infringement of freedom of the press.

The media are seldom given the credit they deserve for being such prominent players in the sports enterprise. Too frequently sports administrators just wish these "know nothings" would simply go away so that sport could be restored to the coaches and athletes. That is wishful thinking, for it will never happen. The genie is out of the bottle. The task is now one of allowing it to perform its magic.

The media cannot do much for women's sports until such time that writers and commentators are educated into the rich possibilities that exist there. The women's sports community has a selling job to do. Changes cannot be achieved overnight. The writers on women's sports beats will need to be jolted from their typical mainstream modes of evaluating the activity if they are to pick up the subtle and profound differences in the ways women approach sport. It is not enough that women simply get more coverage. They need the type of coverage that will judge women athletes and their competition on a broader range of criteria than is customarily employed by writers trained in the ways of the Culture of Conquest.

The media cannot be written off as uninformed and disinterested parties, even if they behave that way, but instead must be recruited as allies in the production of quality sports experiences. It would be most helpful if more women commentators were recruited who could help interpret for the viewers, listeners, and readers those special qualities of sport for women. In tennis, the commentary of Chris Evert, Virginia Wade, and other retired stars is an indication that "her standpoint" is now being given expression. Sports fans in a new age need to hear these informed, gentle but firm, voices. It is also refreshing to see women employed as commentators for men's sporting events, even though some of them, in their efforts to become "one of the boys" forget to allow their feminine side to be revealed. Wouldn't it be refreshing if these women would take advantage of the privileged positions they enjoy to imbue sports with their natural feminine predisposition by focusing attention on the aesthetics of sport rather than upon who is winning and who is losing? If this were to occur, sports fan could learn to enjoy a fuller range of possibilities from their sports experiences. Before too long, the day will come when women commentators are liberated enough to give expression to the unique qualities that they, as women, bring to sport. This will probably not occur until more women are in control rooms, editorial rooms, and most importantly the board rooms of the networks and publishing houses. Then women sports casters and writers will feel free to just be themselves. When that occurs we will know that a creative synthesis has been achieved, one that is providing more men and women with quality sports experiences.

Recently, I was encouraged by report filed by a male Houston Chronicle sports writer, Fran Blinbury, in his column after the Houston Comets had made a remarkable comeback in the second game of the 1998 WNBA playoffs. He reported with great enthusiasm "Quibble with the basketball, if you must. But I've got news for you. Val Ackerman's WNBA product is more fun, more entertaining, more alive than David Stern's game."[7] (Ackerman is commissioner of the WNBA and Stern is commissioner of the NBA) I could not agree more. As a fan and regular witness of both leagues I find the women's league to be reflective of the best of the men's and women's sports traditions. This is indeed good news for those of us who celebrate each and every tiny step toward achieving reform in the world of sport.

How should athletes relate to gender mates?

His standpoint: Gender mates are buddies who protect one another's interests.

Her standpoint: Gender mates are allies who join together to establish their rights, but also are antagonists who compete for the attention of men.

Their standpoint: Gender mates work together to understand their own and the other gender's viewpoint and predicaments.

Sport has become a primary arena in which boys learn to become men. Sports training has become a rite of passage for many young men where they can demonstrate that they are worthy of membership in the club of privilege shared by other males. Some feminist critics see sport as serving as a vehicle for preserving an oppressive patriarchal system. They assert that since women have not had access to the "secrets" of the sports fraternity, that endow their members with special privileges, women have been condemned to second class citizenship. There is no doubt but that sport has traditionally drawn boundaries between men and women. Men have been taught to believe that only their buddies can truly understand their passion for sport. Watch the current crop of sitcoms and observe just how frequently sport is pointed out as a barrier between men and women and as a bonding element for men.

Women, on the other hand, have not used sport as a place where they learn to become women. To the contrary, the home is where most women learn what are considered appropriate female sex roles. But women are beginning to understand that their welfare as a group is intimately connected in very real ways with what happens in the gym and on the playing field. If men have been using sport to gain and maintain privilege, then it behooves women to invade the gyms and playing fields and interrupt these limiting traditions. They need to join together as allies to "outwit the culture" as the noted anthropologist, Margaret Mead, was fond of saying, by taking their rightful place in the scheme of things. Women, by investing in the sports enterprise will learn how to play, not only athletic games, but also the games that really count in the economy and polity. The leaders of the women's sports movement understand that a breakthrough can only be accomplished by joining together in support of one another's and their children's athletic development.

At this moment in history, if "her standpoint" is to be given legitimacy by those establishing sports policies and practices, a concerted collective effort by advocates for women's sports will be required. In my judgment, it is important for both men and women to include in their sports programs provisions that allow each to come to a better understanding of the other. The media can assist in this continuing education process. No plan for the re-formation of sport can be complete without provisions for the expression of both masculine and feminine voices. It is essential for each gender to work with the media to better understand their own and the other's positions. When that occurs, then a synthesis of these two standpoints can be achieved and a creative solution to sports policy dilemmas can be discovered.

How should athletes relate to their bodies?

His standpoint: Ones body is a tool to be used.

Her standpoint: Ones body is a temple to be worshipped, if it meets the rigid standards established by the fashion industry, or if not a vessel to be despised.

Their standpoint: Ones body is a source of pleasure and should be respected, enjoyed, and used with care.

American popular culture pays a lot of attention to the human form, particularly the female form. All kinds of products and programs have been brought onto the scene by the sports and fitness industry to help both men and women conform to their respective ideals. Not only are there elaborate body shaping programs, but also diet clinics that provide clients with weight watching schemes for reforming their bodies. And there are the tanning salons where the body can be brought to just the right color. Then there are the steroids that allow both men and women to sculpt their bodies into fashionable forms. (And let's not forget the silicon that has been used so generously to achieve aesthetic ends.)

These fashions have become intimately linked with the world of sports. It seems safe to conclude that the athletic body, with exaggerated muscle definition, has become the ideal for many involved in the health and fitness movement. Only a few athletes have chosen the more excessive route taken by serious body builders. But the weight control and weight training programs that have been put into effect in nearly all sports training programs for both men and women can be seen as a part of a general social trend toward the masculinization of the body ideal for women. The cover of the 1993 *Sports Illustrated* annual swimsuit edition features a woman who obviously has engaged in significant body building. While there is no mistaking her for a man, the fact that she was chosen as the cover girl reflects the new "hard body" ideal, which is difficult, if not impossible, for the vast majority of women to achieve without long hours in the weight room or without the aid of a generous infusion of testosterone.

This fashion makes clear a major distinction between male and female perspectives on the body and sport. For most men in sport who engage in weight training they are doing it for the purpose of increasing their strength and fitness so that they can better perform their athletic skills. The majority of male athletes are not inclined to sculpture their bodies simply to affirm their masculinity. Most women athletes are also using weight training and weight control as ways to enhance their athletic performance. But for them it is a much more complicated project. Most women in our society are taught to pay a tremendous amount of attention to the shape of their bodies. So much of what occurs in the popular culture draws attention to the female figure. In the media women (and now to some extent men), are being portrayed as sex objects where readers and viewers are constantly being urged to evaluate themselves in relation to the current fashion, which at the moment is tall, thin, and firm.

When athletes enter serious sports training and their coaches choose to put them on diets and weight training, it often exacerbates an already high level of self-consciousness about their physiques. They are regularly reminded by messages from the popular culture of the importance of one's figure in attracting and retaining a mate.

In my playing days, the Charles Atlas body building ads in magazines, showing a weakling having sand kicked in his face, were treated with humor and ridicule. As a matter of fact the world of sports gave little attention to weight training. Coaches in the '40s and '50s were of the opinion that weight training would more than likely reduce effectiveness in executing sports skills. Basketball players were told they would lose their touch. Today both weight control and strength training are acknowledged as essential by nearly all serious male and female athletes.

It can be concluded that from "his standpoint" the body is seen as an instrument to be used in the accomplishment of sports tasks, whereas from "her standpoint" the view is far more confusing. While women do understand that their bodies need to be prepared for accomplishing sports tasks, they also believe that a "good" body is critical to establishing intimate relationships with men. The preoccupation of all women, athletes and non-athletes alike, with how their body looks and smells, causes them to relate to their bodies differently from men. Scrapes, cuts, and bruises that are considered badges of courage for men are often seen by women as blemishes that need to be covered up for fear that they will detract from their sex appeal. Men are much more inclined to risk their bodies in athletic endeavors, sometimes recklessly, which results in unnecessary injuries. In fact, in some instances they are encouraged to do so by their coaches and the sports traditions they are attempting to uphold. Women too are often times urged to sacrifice their bodies, that is, by playing hurt, for the good of the team. Women are generally less inclined to make these sacrifices. For many women sport is not important enough for them to take significant risks for the good of the team.

In my view, the prospects for a synthesis of masculine and feminine perspectives on the body any time in the near future seem slim, indeed. I come to this conclusion because of the powerful influences from the popular culture that young women experience. The good news, however, resides in the questions that are beginning to be raised about both the use of steroids as well as the damaging consequences of the obsession with the ritualistic measuring of body fat in women athletes. In both cases the message that has been communicated to women athletes was in order to maximize athletic performance they had to take on the appearance of men. Presently, sports federations and athletic administrators are more closely monitoring their coaches and athletes to insure that their training practices are not causing physical problems as a result of poorly conceived body development programs. The alarming incidence of eating disorders among women athletes has alerted sports educators to the physical and psychological consequences of some widely employed training fashions.

Hopefully, as time passes and society's definition of the ideal feminine form is expanded to include shapes that do not fit the restrictive aesthetic standards of today, it will become possible for a radically new standpoint to come into being, one that encourages both men and women to treat their bodies as sources of joy to be used with care. The disabling consequences of abusing one's body in the service of achieving athletic objectives must be brought to a halt. In this case, neither "her perspective" nor "his perspective" on the human body contain the elements of reason that are required to bring sanity into sports. It appears that it will be necessary for some outside agent, possibly a regulatory body, to communicate to coaches and athletes that they are currently on a risky and unproductive course. Possibly parents of athletes who are uneasy with the excesses that are developing will take initiatives to bring a halt to high risk training practices, so that athletes will begin to display greater respect for their bodies.

How should athletes view themselves?

His standpoint: You are what you accomplish.

Her standpoint: You are who you associate with.

Their standpoint: You achieve your identity through all of your connections with the world, both through tasks and in relationships with other people.

Athletic achievement is a prominent source of identity for many males in American society. While accomplishments in sport also help women establish their identity there are usually other more central connections with the world that form their conception of who they are. The people with whom they are intimately associated, their family, friends, and potential mates play a prominent role in establishing a self image. It is not inconsequential that women nearly always take on the family name of their mates. They are who they associate with as well as what they accomplish. It is one of the struggles for modern women to overcome this cultural bias. In order to retain dignity they need to define themselves by their accomplishments, as well as by their social connections.

Likewise, it is a tremendous burden for men to be defined primarily by their accomplishments. Without being winners in all sectors of their lives it is difficult for many men to feel good about themselves. This is a case where it would seem truly beneficial for both men and women to expand the means by which they define themselves. The enterprise of sport strongly pushes both men and women toward defining themselves in relation to their achievements. There are few forces in the athletic setting that push athletes toward defining themselves in relation to the people with whom they associate. In this sense sport is primarily a masculine activity.

The question is, "Does it need to remain that way?" Is it possible for sport to place less emphasis upon outcomes and more on processes? Quite candidly, it would take some major modifications in the ways sports are conducted to change the current emphasis. Sport is a performing art and is judged by how well the performance is executed. While it is possible to broaden the criteria used to judge an effective performance to include aesthetic and community development dimensions, the fact remains that it is most frequently the scoreboard that is used by athletes and spectators alike to judge the activity. Outcomes loom large.

These observations suggest that "his standpoint" is supported by the very nature of the activity itself. Any changes that would bring sport more in line with "her standpoint" would require major transformations in how society views sports experiences. If sport is viewed from a socio-cultural perspective where it is seen as performing important community building functions, then it may be possible for it to lean more in the direction of "her standpoint" as it would if aesthetic dimensions were given greater emphasis. It should not be necessary for women to define themselves in the same manner as men for them to be able to feel good about themselves while having a sports experience. Ultimately, it may be possible for both men and women athletes to achieve their identity through all of their connections with the world, including the sports tasks they undertake and the people with whom they identify. It is limiting when either tasks or relationships are used exclusively as focal points for identity. Such limitations are revealed in "Old Jocks" who are never able to move on to defining themselves in new ways after their playing days have come to an end. (See Chapter 6) Limitations are also found among those women who are never encouraged to engage in the serious development of a performance skill that can be tested and used as a feature of their self definition. Women, if they are to be liberated from current cultural constraints, need to be able to view themselves as competent achievers as well as loyal care givers. And men need to be freed from defining themselves primarily in relation to their achievements.

The experience of grandfathering has, for many of my contemporaries, become the first time in their lives that they have felt free to define themselves in terms of their relationships rather than in terms of their achievements. It is sad to realize that it has taken these former jocks six decades to develop the care-giving side of themselves. They were either too busy or too tied up in their own identity struggles when they had their own children to allow themselves the joys of giving care and defining themselves in that way. Wouldn't it be enriching if we could discover a way, when men are in their formative years, to give them permission to develop the caring side of themselves? Transforming sport in ways that places greater emphasis upon processes and relationships rather than upon outcomes and tasks could be one way to introduce men to their tender, caring side so that they can find new ways to increase the possibilities for joy and satisfaction.

How should athletes relate to their intimates?

His standpoint: One should not risk self disclosure.

Her standpoint: It is important to risk self disclosure.

Their standpoint: Self-disclosure is essential for establishing intimacy, but is better expressed in some contexts than in others.

Since men are in competition with one another from a very early age in so many aspects of their lives, they are provided little training in how to develop close relationships with their peers. Therefore, they find it difficult to be self disclosing, a prerequisite to establishing intimacy. They do, of course, bond with their male buddies, but these relationships typically center around the activities that knit them together. In the sports setting male athletes generally impose limits on their interaction with their associates. Any discussion that takes place about their relationships with the women in their lives is couched in such a way that they never have to expose a weakness or an uncertainty. In other words, male athletes are often lonely and have no one with whom to share their innermost thoughts, not unlike most men in America, except that traits of self-sufficiency are often exaggerated in athletes. Since male athletes live under the injunction, "Be a real man," the emotions they experience through their frustrations with sports and daily living generally have to be worked out privately and in an indirect fashion. Sport provides outlets for the inevitable anger and frustration that result when one is constantly faced with having to test oneself as a person, student, and as an athlete. This frustration and anger finds expression on the playing field in legitimate aggressive acts, whether it be in tackling an opponent or swinging away at a ball. The locker room also provides outlets for the verbal expression of these repressed emotions. Most male athletes get relief from pent-up frustration through the constant exchange of friendly verbal jabs. It is a "man's way" of relieving tension and bonding with those peers with whom they interact on a regular basis. The bonding that takes place is achieved through the development of shared meanings, not through the exchange of personal "secrets."

In contrast, women athletes are trained from the time they are little girls to provide one another and the men in their lives with emotional support when frustration or anger are experienced. They too develop shared meanings, but more often these meanings derive from the common experiences they have in attempting to establish close relationships with the men and women in their lives. Locker room exchanges between women are usually focused more on relationships, about their personal experiences with the coach, other players, roommates and boyfriends rather than on the tasks, statistics, and outcomes of sport. As women, they are expected to display their sensitivity to those around them. If one of their friends has experienced a setback in a practice or game, they more often than not assume responsibility for aiding in the recovery. In the main, men do no more than pat a dispirited teammate on the rear and move on to other issues that will relieve them both of having to deal with their feelings. Neither the injured party nor his supporter take the occasion to express directly their feelings of failure on the one hand or their feelings of empathy on the other. In most cases they move on as quickly as possible to a topic that is not emotionally charged.

Both of these two standpoints are limiting. Men are forced to carry, throughout their lives, a lot of emotional baggage as a result of their constant repression of their feelings of failure and inadequacy. Women, on the other hand, are constantly opening themselves up to the possibility that one of their confidants will take advantage of their candor to further aggravate a festering wound. Both of these styles are limiting to the athletes if they use only one or the other approach to dealing with the normal frustrations of life in their respective sports communities.

Coaches can take actions that exacerbate these traditional approaches to self disclosure. Coaches of men basically communicate to their charges that they do not want the playing field cluttered with emotional debris. Their athletes are taught to "leave that crap at the gym door." Coaches of women, on the other hand, quite frequently make a genuine effort to get the athlete's feelings out in the open so that they can be dealt with in ways that will not intrude onto the playing field. Clearly "her standpoint" is radically different from "his standpoint."

This difference in men's and women's styles of dealing with their sentiments becomes most evident when men coach women. It is difficult for most male coaches to adopt a style of relating to their women athletes that accommodates the feminine predisposition to be self-disclosing. Also it is extremely important for most women athletes to be accepted as total human beings, not simply as athletic performers, which makes the task of a male coach all the more difficult, for he is generally unprepared for picking up expressions of need on the part of his athletes.

The differences in standpoints are at the moment quite distinct. There is evidence in the larger culture that these masculine and feminine predispositions may be gradually growing together. The tough and the tender are achieving a synthesis in more and more New Generation men and women. But at the moment there is little evidence in the cultures of men's and women's sports that such a synthesis is occurring to any great extent. A few men in sports are becoming more capable of being self-disclosing. However, it appears that while the numbers are still small, more women are becoming less dependent on their traditional style of securing emotional nourishment.

When men and women learn through their experiences that there are times when self-disclosure is growth-enhancing and times when it is counterproductive, they will be better able to discover a fuller range of human possibilities. Sport could become a good arena in which to accomplish this synthesis of his and her standpoints. Whether the social forces are in place at the moment to achieve a synthesis in either men's or women's sports remains to be seen. Unfortunately, changes that take place in the popular culture are often times slow to reach the playing field.

My prediction is that a synthesis will be achieved much more quickly in women's sports than in men's sports, simply because it is far more difficult to learn to become self disclosing than it is to learn when it is most appropriate to be self disclosing. Furthermore, I understand that there are many more powerful social forces prescribing restraint in self disclosure than there are dictating a new openness. But hope resides in the fact that the new age is ushering in a level of candor and openness that has never before been experienced in American life.

How should athletes relate to people unlike themselves?

His standpoint: Invest in your own groups, but be tolerant and fair.

CREATIVE TENSION

Her standpoint: Show concern for everyone.

Their standpoint: Invest in your own group, but demonstrate tolerance and concern for others, especially those less fortunate than you.

Athletes are one of the most sheltered groups in our society. They spend so many hours each day either going to school, training, or competing that they have little opportunity to interact with people different from themselves, unless, of course, their team is ethnically and economically diverse. Even when teams are culturally diverse their common bond to sport often times makes the team members more alike than different. At the collegiate level it has been estimated that athletes spend at least as much time on their athletics as they do on their academics. The balance of their time is often spent at social gatherings where they are again exclusively with their fellow athletes. This is typically a context in which male athletes are encouraged to be tolerant of differences and to be fair in their dealings with one another, whatever their differences might be.

Women athletes, on the other hand, have been trained to "keep their antennae up" so that they can be prepared to go to the aide of anyone in need. Women athletes are more likely than men athletes to sense injustice or disadvantage in any situations in which they find themselves. But again, the schedule of training and competition for most serious women athletes is so demanding that they seldom come into contact with people different from themselves.

Outsiders, that is, people whose life experiences are radically different from those of the athlete, are nearly always a feature of each sportscape. These are the people in each community who the athletes may encounter, but with whom they have little interaction. Since their experiences with outsiders are limited, it would be valuable for athletes to become more sensitive to their unique predicaments. Coming to an awareness of the special needs of people different from them allows athletes to discover new possibilities within themselves and within their situations. Attitudes of tolerance and fairness, while desirable, do not necessarily result in the discovery of new possibilities. A genuine concern for the welfare of others, especially those less fortunate than the athletes themselves, could, however, result in experiences of empowerment for the athletes and enlivenment of their communities.

In this case "her standpoint" is one that is more likely to serve the interests of the athletes and their communities. In fact, on some college campuses athletes are currently urged, and in some cases required, to invest in communities-in-need by coaching, counseling, and/or tutoring young people. Such activities are mutually empowering. The children in these neighborhoods have the advantage of being in the presence of an achieving young person who can serve as a model, while the athletes are provided opportunities to develop their social conscience and understanding of others.

While "her standpoint" on the issue of developing community responsibility seems to be the most growth enhancing, the fact remains that athletic life is exceptionally cloistered. Athletes are insulated and isolated from the realities of life beyond the gym walls. I have discovered among college athletes, both male and female, that they do not regularly read a daily newspaper or even routinely watch television news. They claim they have no time. But there are a few athletes who are not limited by these isolating practices, which suggests that it is the norms of the athletic culture as much as the constraints on time that isolate athletes from the community. It seems important for everyone's welfare that athletes go beyond tolerance, fairness, and concern and be urged to invest themselves in their communities for both their own and their community's welfare.

By achieving a synthesis of the male and female standpoints athletes could be inspired to expand their horizons and exercise community responsibility. In my view, "her voice" will have to be raised to a high pitch in order to put out a call for action by athletes that reflect a heightened social consciousness. If the athletes, male and female, can begin by investing in getting to know and supporting those members of their team who are different from themselves, the team would become a stronger springboard for launching them into the larger community where their resourcefulness could be drawn upon to make the world a kinder and gentler place.

After comparing typical masculine and feminine perspectives on sport, it is evident that in far too many cases neither of these traditional approaches is in tune with what is needed by young people or by the communities in which they live. It seems abundantly clear that the "investors" in both men's and women's sports, that is, the athletes, their families, their coaches, community policy makers, and corporate sponsors, all need to be challenged to reevaluate those policies and practices currently in place. A thoughtful analysis of the issues introduced here should lead one to conclude that far too much of what is currently happening in sport is neither good for the athletes, their communities, nor for that matter, the sports enterprise itself. Men and women must vigorously search for a common ground upon which to build a foundation for a cultural renaissance in sport.

Counterpoint

CHAPTER NINE

Sports for Tomorrow:
The Culture of Counterpoint

The invasion of women into the world of sport over the past quarter century since the enactment of Title IX is inviting us to "change the game." There seems to be no question that we are in the process of changing the nature of sport, if only so slightly. New Generation men and women are taking initiatives to bring about change in all of our social institutions, including sport.

Throughout this book I have been arguing that the values young girls bring into sports from their upbringing as women, in what I have been calling the Culture of Care, are challenging male-oriented values that have been a part of the traditional Culture of Conquest which has defined the meaning of sport for so long. I have been presenting evidence and testimony in support of the proposition that we are observing a dialectic where a synthesis between these two perspectives on sport will occur and will guide sports policies and practices in the decades ahead. I have used the concept of counterpoint to describe the merging of the traditional male and female perspectives on sport. Why counterpoint?

Two of my favorite legends in the music world are J.S. Bach, the master of 18th century music, and contemporary jazz artist Dave Brubeck. I've asked myself why I find Baroque music and improvisational jazz, two distinctly different art forms from two radically different eras, so attractive. My guess is that I am inspired by these two musical traditions because both employ a structure that combines separate melodic lines to create a wonderful rich texture. Counterpoint allows independent voices to follow their own course, but at the same time to be combined in ways that create very special musical moments. Clearly, the sum is greater than the parts. There is a synergy, or a state of mutual enhancement, between the musicians performing each melody. This creative cooperation between the various voices is most evident when witnessing a live concert. Not only do the artists play off one another, but the energy and mood created by one artist allows the others to rise to higher levels of performance and creativity. Each performance yields a new interpretation. When these forms of music are performed well, they uplift the spirits, not only of the artists, but also of all the listeners. How wonderful it is to witness these very special performances.

Is it possible that directors of sports activities can decide upon a structure for their performances that allow them to achieve these same ends, that is, moments of creative cooperation, awe, and wonder? I think so. Synergy can be created in the sports arena, just as it can in the music hall.

How would we recognize a synergistic athletic moment if we experienced one? These special moments occur when all of the participants feel a sense of excitement as they combine their separate efforts to create something that is more than what one of them could achieve by themselves. The participants sense energy being passed from one person to another, from athlete to athlete, from coach to athlete, from spectator to athlete, etc. These kinds of athletic moments can only occur when the various actors are carefully prepared for the experience and free to express their unique selves. Counterpoint can occur only when each voice has its unique melody and style.

The Culture of Conquest and the Culture of Care each has a voice that carries distinctive melodies and styles. If the voices articulating these different cultural perspectives work together to create a structure in which they can perform comfortably together, it will be possible to create very special athletic moments. For this to occur, however, it will be necessary for the orchestrators of these performances to audition the full range of voices that appear in the sports arenas. We need more than an all-tenor performance such as the one featuring Domingo, Cararras, and Pavaroti, as elegant as their concerts have been. Without well-modulated female voices it will be difficult to create music that enlivens us all as we enter this new era.

Yesterday, when the Culture of Conquest was an all male choir, sport preserved male privilege. Today, as the voices of the Culture of Care are beginning to be heard, new possibilities are presenting themselves, where sport is becoming a source of empowerment and enlivenment for both men and women. While most of the voices from the Culture of Care are female, more and more males are being attracted to their New Generation "music." Tomorrow will see the results of a blending of these two voices. The result will be a new perspective on sport, where the voices of yesterday and today are combined in ways that create a new texture which is richer and more attuned to the needs and tastes of men and women as they enter the 21st century.

One of the major needs of men and women as they enter the next century is to create a sanctuary where they can be inspired and renewed. This sanctuary must be free from the ugliness of everyday life, if it is to perform its renewal functions. Sport can become such a sanctuary, if men and women work together to create a structure that is composed of the best of the cultures of conquest and care. A synthesis of these two cultures can lead to new policies and practices that allow sport to effectively perform its renewal functions.

Stephen Covey, author of *The 7 Habits of Highly Effective People*, and other best sellers, has asked the following question:

> Could synergy not create a new script for the next generation-one that is more geared to service and contribution, and less protective, less adversarial, less selfish; one that is more open, more trusting, more giving, and less defensive, protective, and political; one that is more loving, more caring, and is less possessive and judgmental.[1]

Covey is inviting us to write a script, or to stay with our musical metaphor, a libretto, that places greater emphasis upon the Culture of Care with his call for more openness, trust, giving, loving, and caring and less of those characteristics associated with the excesses of the Culture of Conquest. Throughout this book I have been asking the question whether we might be able to create a new script for sport that represents a synthesis that brings into being a new Culture of Counterpoint where the values Covey prizes are given greater prominence. I have come to believe that a common ground can be found in sport where men and women are mutually enhanced by opening up to one another's values. Yesterday's battleground can become tomorrow's common ground.

I have become increasingly convinced that the most fruitful way to arrive at enlightened sports policies and practices is to focus upon the ways sports experiences can synergize all participants, athletes, coaches, parents, event managers, and spectators. If we fail to incorporate any of the voices in our composition, we will be limiting the amount of synergy, or creative cooperation that can be generated. Resistance anywhere will negatively affect the extent to which synergy occurs.

Sports experiences that produce creative cooperation, not only renew the spirits of individual participants, but enliven the groups to which the participants belong. These special experiences also break down barriers and bridge the distance between classes of individuals: men and women, black and white, rich and poor, etc.

Critics of sport who focus exclusively upon its impact on individuals fail to understand how sport affects the welfare of both face-to-face groups and classes of individuals. Classes, such as women, African-Americans, and the economically disenfranchised, as well as face-to-face groups, such as friendship, family, work, and school groups, can be enlivened and empowered by sport when they and their values are admitted into the rites of renewal. The rituals of sport are most invigorating when they reflect the values of all participating groups, not only the values of achievement-oriented males. The latter could benefit by incorporating into their sports programs some of the values of those groups and classes of individuals who have traditionally been excluded from policy-making in sport. The admission of these disenfranchised groups into the mainstream is bringing new dimensions of richness and vitality to the sports experience. A systems-centered approach allows new opportunities for enlivenment to be incorporated into the sports experience, provoking a new synergy.

My observation is that conventional sports programs are neither principle, person, power, nor systems-centered, but instead are masculine achievement centered. They are dominated by the values of the Culture of Conquest. Too frequently the traditions of male sports dictate the policies and practices that govern all training and competition. Little attention is given to the needs of young people, or to the requirements of the social units or classes to which they belong. A systems-centered approach attends to the needs of all participants, giving special attention to the requirements of friendship groups, families, work groups, neighborhoods, schools, and communities as well as to the social classes to which the participants belong. The purpose of what I am calling Connective Sports is not only to achieve personal renewal, but also to revitalize and strengthen the groups to which the participants belong, especially the family, while attending to the special needs of women. It is my conclusion that carefully constructed sports programs can strengthen group ties, help overcome barriers between men and women, as well as promote individual renewal. On the other hand, poorly conceived programs can destroy the spirits of participants, create diminished cohesiveness in the participant's social groupings, and further exacerbate class divisions and disadvantages, widening rather than bridging the distance.

Gender, racial, ethnic, and economic discrimination compromise access to the benefits of sport for far too many Americans. Sport has had a long history of discrimination against certain classes of individuals, since resources have not, and are not, equally accessible to everyone. Women have had less access to resources than men. African-Americans and Hispanics have less access to opportunity than whites. And the children of the poor have less access to quality sports training than the rich. While, over the years, there have been gains made by all of these classes of individuals, the gap between them is still frustratingly great.

There is an illusion of equal access created by the presence of a few highly visible African-American professional athletes from lower economic origins who have become prominent public figures. There are some high profile women athletes who give the illusion that women have access to opportunities in sport. The fact remains that opportunities are not equal for any of the disenfranchised classes in spite of how it appears. While most poor people have access to sports on TV, many cannot afford a ticket to enjoy a live professional or college sports event. While many sports superstars are African-American or Hispanic there is still less access to sports training for minority youth. And while there are women athletes who have become household names, the numbers are few and opportunities for women are restricted at all levels. There is much less to celebrate at sports events where classes of one's fellow citizens are excluded for whatever reasons.

It is not only unjust for classes of individuals to have less opportunity for sports experiences, but the absence of diversity limits the benefits that can be taken from the sports experience. Having the opportunity to connect with someone who is different, to be able to bridge the distance to that person can have a renewing effect. Interacting with like individuals is less of a challenge, therefore, less enlivening. Gender, racial, cultural, and economic diversity add to the richness of the sports experience. At the international level we seem to understand that, for it is a part of the rhetoric justifying the Olympic Games, the Goodwill Games, and other international competitions. But at the domestic level sports leaders seem less interested in taking advantage of the benefits of cultural diversity. Sports programs at the community level are often as segregated as the neighborhoods in which athletes

COUNTERPOINT

live. Sport, more than most other institutions, offers a ready-made context for using cultural diversity to empower and enliven participants. Sports reform needs to be a part of our national agenda for advancing opportunity for disenfranchised groups. Fortunately, some of the leading sporting goods manufacturers are coming to an understanding of the need to provide equal access to sports resources. For example, Nike has put into place their P.L.A.Y. program (Participate in the Lives of America's Youth) with the goal of increasing sports opportunities for everyone, regardless of social origins. Without a doubt, everyone wins when corporations make such an investment. Young people are provided with more opportunities, their families and communities are enriched by their sports experiences, and the sporting goods manufacturers sell more products. This is an encouraging example of creative cooperation at work. Women, minorities, and the economically disadvantaged all benefit from such programs. However, if a concerted effort is not made to give these new voices a prominent role in the mainstream culture of sport, synergy will not be created and all parties will fail to get the most out of their sports experiences. Being together is not enough. It is essential that provisions be made to allow values of the out-group to impact sports policies and practices. The participants have to be allowed to show respect for what each brings to these renewal rites. Renewal is more likely to occur if there is something new added to the mix.

Ken Burns, the director of the 18-hour PBS documentary on the history of baseball, makes this observation:

This [the history of baseball] is the story of immigration and assimilation, as each wave of immigrants sought the permanent status of citizenship conveyed, not by a piece of paper, but by participation in the national pastime of their adopted land. First it was the Irish, then the Germans, the Poles and other Central Europeans. Then it was the Italians, the Greeks, belatedly the Africans, then the Latins and Asians, each group invigorating the game as they have our country's dynamic social fabric.[2]

Over the decades, new groups have been able to imprint spectacle sport with their culture and have been able to use sport as a vehicle for assimilation.

I do firmly believe that when more diversity occurs in our sports programs for young people, all participants will be enriched. In the meantime, when Connective Sports principles are applied to athletic activities, regardless of whether these activities are culturally integrated, opportunities are provided for all participants to be re-energized. With this new found energy they can, if they are so inclined, invest in the politics of achieving both gender equity and gender synergy. We do not have to await a social revolution to enjoy uplifting sports experiences. Nor should we be quieted because a value we hold dear is not currently allowed expression through our lives in sport. Sport is enriched when all participants are provided opportunities to assert themselves to achieve parity for their special values.

In short, sport does not need to be a zero sum game, where one person's gain is another person's loss. Everyone can leave the sports arena a winner if the time and effort is invested in creating experiences where resources are mobilized so that all participants can be inspired by their experiences together. Men and women must transform the battleground into a common ground, or if you will, a playground, where they can join together to uplift one another's spirits.

Where can those who wish to create a more gender-just world find allies to infuse the culture of sport with values that make experiences on the playing field more civil, aesthetic, and connective? Without the support of activist fathers it will be impossible to reshape sport so that it is in greater sync with the requirements of a society where men and women treat one another with dignity and mutual respect.

Naomi Wolf in *Fire With Fire* observes:

> Fathers, brothers, sons, lovers, husbands, friends: All the men who care about the women in their lives are, whether they know it or not, male feminists. And they deserve better than caricatures and dismissal. They deserve their place alongside women in the discussion of how to heal the gender divide, and make public life fairer for their daughters and home life more compelling for their sons.[3]

My experiences in working with fathers of young women athletes give me reason to be encouraged. I have even seen hard-nosed, victory-obsessed coaches who have become fathers reassess their typical warrior approaches to sport when their own daughters began their sports careers. Before they changed roles from being a coach to being a concerned parent they had little reason to reconsider their comfortable command and control methods of coaching. Also, when dads who are not coaches, but who are very deeply entrenched in the mainstream culture of sport, witness their daughters' struggles on the playing field, they quickly come to understand that all is not right with the institution of sport. They learn very soon that sports education opportunities available to their daughters are not equivalent to those available to their sons. It is not unusual for some fathers to be inspired to take another look at the whole sports enterprise and to conclude that all of sport would be better off if women were allowed to imprint it with their feminine nurturer-connector values.

I have to admit, however, that there are many men who demand that their daughters "suck it up" and adopt the warrior mentality, come hell or high water. Those zealous parents are either the coach's dream or their worst nightmare. They are a dream when they loyally support the coach's traditional policies and practices. They are a nightmare when they try to get into the act and impose their warrior ways directly on their daughter, the team, or the coach. These zealous warriors are the ones who often attempt to tell the coaches how to do their jobs.

I have no solid data about what percentage of the dads are "challengers" to the conventional sports ideology, or how many are "supporters" of traditional approaches, or how many are "zealots" who support warrior ways with a vengeance. My experiences with hundreds of dads over the past 20 years would tell me that the supporters of Culture of Conquest sports ideology are in the majority, with the zealots being next in numbers, and with the challengers to the traditional male sports ideology a small minority. I see all fathers on a continuum from challenging traditions on the left to zealously supporting traditions on the right, with the vast majority of fathers of young women athletes distributed in the middle of a bell-shaped curve, expressing various levels of support for traditional male sports values. Most are prepared to say "yes, but" to traditional sports training for their daughters—yes, but not if she has to suffer indignities from a crazy coach; yes, but not at the expense of her academic development; yes, but not if she has to play hurt or ill; yes, but not if she has to miss traditional family gatherings for sports training or competition; yes, but not if her parents cannot share in the experience; yes, but not if she cannot spend time with her boyfriend, etc. These "yes, buts" are the reservations that reformers can tap into in developing alliances with this large group of middle of the road fathers.

Clearly, "challengers" are ready-made allies for sports reform.

They simply need a forum in which to clarify the issues, identify strategies for change, and find support for their newly discovered perspective on sport. They have examined the "yes, buts" and made a determination that all is not well with mainstream sports traditions. They simply have to be assured that there are other "real men" out there who share their sentiments. Then they will be ready to lead the charge.

The "zealots" are probably lost causes, their identity is too tightly wrapped up in the male sports culture for them to be able to participate in sports reform in any significant way. They often live miserable lives as they witness their daughters' experiences with sport, unless, of course, their daughters turn out to be superstars. Even then, as has been shown in the case of tennis star, Mary Pierce, and others, zealous fathers suffer greatly. Besides, they turn out to be embarrassing and annoying to their daughters and to nearly everyone within earshot. In spite of the fact that the large majority of fathers are enthusiastic supporters of the Culture of Conquest, they are still promising candidates for being nudged to the left. While few of these dads are prepared to express concern about what is happening to their sons on the playing field, many appear to be ready to take issue when their daughters are mistreated or disadvantaged. We need to remember that many of these fathers were college-age participants in the cultural revolution of the '60s and are not aliens to the values of the Culture of Care. Furthermore, they are likely to still be struggling with their relationship with WOMAN that derives from their experiences of being raised by a mother, with all of the complexity that goes with the family drama. Where they are, in the resolution of this conflict, will influence how ready they are to embrace Culture of Care values and join in reform efforts.

Abusive coaching techniques are seen by more than a few fathers as doing violence to their daughters. These same techniques might be viewed by these fathers as "building character" in their sons. While fathers with double standards may not be attractive allies to feminist reformers, they are at least open to reevaluating current sports policies and practices. They do not have to pass a political test in order to participate in sports reform. Most of that middle group probably feel more than a slight tinge of discomfort with what they are observing. They have been offered a glimpse of what quality sports experiences can be while witnessing their daughter's sports activities. But they too need clarification, exposure to alternative strategies for change, and support from other dads and moms, if they are to assume an activist stance.

These potential challengers need permission from their daughters to get involved in reform efforts. Permission is often difficult to secure, since teenage girls do not want to be perceived as being different. They certainly do not want their friends to think they are being controlled by their parents. Fathers need to learn skills for securing permission from their daughters so that they can take an active stance in bringing more sanity to sport.

Equity issues are those around which nearly all dads can be rallied, whether they are challengers, supporters, or zealots. No father wants his daughter to get the short end of the stick. Some may be more concerned about their sons coming up short than their daughters, but most want all their children to have the best. In my experience the equity feminist agenda is not difficult to sell to most of these dads, especially when they think that the shortfall might reduce their daughters' chances for a college scholarship! A relationship of mutual trust with fathers can be based upon the foundation of sports equity issues.

It is when traditional Culture of Conquest values are challenged by reformers that many fathers get edgy. So much of their sex role identity is tied up in the mainstream sports culture. However, when warrior coaching techniques are viewed as doing violence to their daughter's confidence and self-esteem, many angry fathers can be rallied to action, whatever their history of connection with the mainstream culture of sport. However, the breaking point varies from father to father. Some fathers are not alarmed until their daughter announces she intends to quit the team. Others die a slow death each time their daughter is violated by a harsh word from a coach. The latter are more likely to become allies for reform. The former have difficulty acknowledging that the cultural values they have lived with for their entire lives are the cause of their daughter's discontent. They tend to blame the victim, their daughter, rather than blame the system or the coach. That is an outcome that neither helps their daughters, nor contributes to the enhancement of the institution of sport.

Most of today's mothers are feminists whether or not they identify themselves as such. Deep inside the psyches of nearly all modern American women is a clear sense of what is fair, just, and civilized.

Many of them do not know how to give voice to these sentiments, but nearly all of them sense that the status quo is not right and that changes need to be made. What goes on in sport for their sons and daughters does not always conform to their sense of right and wrong. But too often they do not feel confident in their knowledge of sport or confident to express themselves in an arena where they personally have had little experience. Furthermore, many of them are prepared to yield to their husbands in matters of sport because men claim expertise in that area. Some single mothers have nowhere to turn for guidance. These limitations, however, do not rule out most mothers as allies in the sports reform movement. Their greatest asset is that they have been socialized into the Culture of Care. They know nurturance and they know connection. These values can be the foundation for building an alliance with sports reformers.

Alliances cannot be forged by assaults on the character and life styles of those women who the feminist leaders are attempting to recruit. Riki Robbins Jones in *The Empowered Woman* expresses concern that the feminist leaders have tried to pin a label on women when the essence of women lies in their incredible diversity. She observes that:

> Not all of us are career persons. Each and every one of us experiences unique struggles, choices, and personal transitions that do not fit into any single stereotype. We want to find our own way without being told by anyone, including the feminists, what we "should" do.[4]

Each mother of an athlete has chosen a distinctive life style. But they are united by the fact of motherhood and of being raised as a woman in a society where sex discrimination has, at some point in each of their lives, presented them with frustrating barriers. Many of these mothers are angry, some are raging, and some are out of touch with reality. Their experiences with the institution of sport have left most of them with concerns that have provoked at least some degree of anger. Few mothers have not at one point or another wanted to take their child out of harms way. A mother cannot watch her child compete on the playing field without experiencing some anger at those who stand in the way of her child's fulfillment. A mother's close connection with the Culture of Care, her pain of being discriminated against because of her gender, and her experiences of trying to keep her children free of the consequences of humiliation and failure make her a prime candidate for building alliances for change.

Presently, mothers have few forums for articulating their concerns about sports policies and practices. Typically, their husbands are unable to see the world from their standpoint, because they are so enmeshed in the mainstream culture of sport. Furthermore, they have too few opportunities to share their concerns with other mothers. Sports reformers have overlooked a large cadre of potential allies in this group of mothers. Few mothers are comfortable witnessing their sons getting smashed up in the manly sports. And no mother likes to see either her son or daughter lose self-confidence and self-esteem at the hands of an abusive coach. Parents want to think that the leaders of sports programs for their children are just as concerned about their child's physical and psychological well being as they are. Seldom is that the case, for these leaders have their own agendas. Too frequently the warrior values dominate in sports training and competition, at the exclusion of traditional feminine values. Many mothers have difficulty relating to these values, especially as they are applied to the education of their daughters. Unfortunately, most women who administer sports programs for women have bought into mainstream sports culture values. Too many have left their Culture of Care values at the door in an effort to gain acceptance from the male sports leadership. Of course, that outcome is not all bad. Young women need to be exposed to the best of the warrior's ways, and a caring woman can temper masculine values with a feminine touch. But female coaches are frequently not individuals with whom mothers can identify and in whom they can confide their concerns about what they see happening on the playing field. Besides, some female coaches push warrior values harder than many males in order to ensure their male supervisors of their commitment to mainstream sports values, or because they have experienced a typical male induction into the culture of sport.

Mothers then are primed to become allies in efforts to infuse sport with traditional feminine values. Because of the sex discrimination they have experienced, because of the impotence they have been made to feel in relation to their husband's sports "expertise," and because of the advanced development of their nurturer-connector self, most mothers are ready to participate in a reevaluation of the conventional wisdom in the world of sport. The leaders of the gender re-assessment movement need to take full advantage of the readiness of this group. This alliance cannot be achieved if these mothers are asked to pass a "political correctness" test in order to join with feminists in sports reform efforts. It is essential that those on the right who oppose abortion, vote against equal rights amendments, challenge the veracity of Anita Hill, and judge O.J. Simpson innocent, be welcomed into the sports reform community as well as the true believers in radical solutions to the problems of gender inequity. Nearly all of the mothers of young athletes share a rootedness in the Culture of Care, nearly all have witnessed their child experience inexcusable personal discounts on the playing field, and most of them see the potential for their children of learning good things through their sports experiences. Most also see sport as a place that can be used to build family unity. They understand that an investment in improving the quality of their children's sports experiences has potential payoff. Most can be convinced to make an investment. Some investments will be small, like raising funds so that their daughter's team can be tested against the very best. Some will be large, where they assume responsibility for creating a sports training program that reflects their value system.

In most situations neither mothers nor fathers are invited by sports leaders to participate in sports policy decision-making. As a matter of fact, professional sports educators make a concerted effort to exclude parents from the decision-making process because they assume parents will act in an irrational, self-serving manner. This prevailing attitude makes it difficult for parents who wish to become activists in sports reform to get a hearing and to leave their mark. If a parent signals an equity concern or challenges the mainstream warrior values, very often they quickly get labeled as either troublemakers or zealous feminists. When this labeling occurs their inputs tend to be discounted. It is almost impossible for an individual parent to ally himself or herself with the feminist agenda without facing angry resistance. This reality of the sportscape must be factored into any effort to build an alliance with fathers and mothers to accomplish a feminist reform agenda.

Not all parents are equally strong candidates for joining in alliances for change in the world of sport. Mothers may be better candidates than fathers. White collar mothers and fathers may feel more comfortable challenging command and control models of

sports leadership, since these parents are more likely to be participants in organizations that have adopted shared decision making pro-
cedures. They also are more likely to have been active participants in
counter cultural challenges when they were in college. Many blue
collar occupations still demand adherence to autocratic policies and
practices and few blue collar men and women were a part of the '60s
protests. The men were in Viet Nam fighting the war. Blue collar
workers are also less likely to be sympathetic to the feminist agenda.

Poor African American parents are also more likely to be focused
upon what sport can do for their children, economically, than upon
women's issues with which many of them cannot identify. Dr.
Jackline Light summarizes the plight of the black mother:

The problems of the feminist movement are not our problems. Black women have
not been oppressed by their men....In a global sense, the problem of the black woman
is to get her man on a level of parity with her: The system has oppressed him. For
most black women, the feminist rhetoric about male oppression is very much beside
the point.[5]

However, the equity issue is one that black men and women can
both relate to when it can be shown that their daughters are not getting access to resources essential for maximizing their futures in
sport. But because of the realities of life in the poor black family
there may very well be economic constraints upon the extent to
which mothers and fathers are able to participate in sports reform
efforts. Also, it is entirely possible that parenting and discipline patterns that black mothers employ are more consistent with traditional
coach-centered approaches in sport. Command and control coaching
strategies, while unappealing to many white middle-class parents,
may appeal to black single mothers as essential for managing their
children in their particular setting. Whether that observation proves
to be the case, it seems probable that the black and white parent's
agendas could very well be different.

Professional sports educators have traditionally been defenders of
the status quo and can be counted upon to vigorously resist initiatives
for change, especially those coming from liberal sources. But some of
those who have been socialized into the mainstream culture of sport
have been touched by forces affecting change in the world beyond the
gym walls. Some sports educators have allowed themselves to be

impacted by the values that are calling for kinder and gentler social policies and practices in all of our social institutions, including sport. While most members of the sports education community have a "pull yourself up by your own bootstraps" approach to overcoming adversity in all aspects of their lives, some find it possible to identify with the disenfranchised and the oppressed. While many women leaders in sport have bought into mainstream social values, some have experienced enough gender discrimination to be receptive to reevaluating conventional wisdom in the world of sport.

My experience with women sports leaders is that they can be mobilized to address equity issues more easily than they can be inspired to challenge male-constructed warrior training traditions. Too many women coaches behave as if it is OK to be verbally abusive of athletes and remain focused exclusively upon the scoreboard. While some women coaches and administrators are too far removed from the values of mainstream women to join an alliance with them, I would like to think that nearly all of them are potential candidates for participation in sports reform dialogue. While in the women's sports community feminism is not as robust as one might expect, women coaches have had the experience of being women in a society that does not always treat women with respect and dignity. Their experiences as a woman make them candidates for joining alliances for change.

A positive force for change is the social climate beyond the gym walls. While it is true that serious sports participants often live in a cocoon of their own making and are too frequently oblivious to what is occurring in "the real world," the inclusion of parents in the mix lets some light shine on the sports enterprise. Parents work and live in social institutions where New Generation values are impacting policies and practices. Before too long many of them will become conscious of the gap that exists between the cultures of their work settings and the culture of sport. Some parents have already taken steps to imprint their children's sports with new values. That is a very positive sign.

Furthermore, as much as coaches might try to isolate athletes from "corrupting" influences, these young people are tied into a larger youth culture that, for better or worse, is influencing their values. Reformers can count upon many young athletes to line up with them in opposition to those sports practices that are out of sync with what is happening "out there" in the rest of the world. The values of the youth culture are being influenced by the same forces that are changing all of our other social institutions.

At every turn I see evidence that the Culture of Care has pervaded the new generation of athletes, both male and female. In April, 1995 *USA Today* published its All-USA boys and girls high school basketball teams. (April 18, 1995, p. 4C and April 20, 1995, p. 10C). For each athlete a short profile was written based upon eight common questions. The answers from both the boys and girls to one of the key questions betrayed a common commitment to New Generation values. When asked "What makes you special?" seven of ten of these high achievers responded with a reference to their relationships to others. One made reference to his "spirituality," one to her "bowlegs and pigeon toes," and one to her work ethic that allowed her to perform better than expected. The seven references to relationships were:

- "I respect people for who they are, not what they do. If I'm your friend, it becomes a special friendship."

- "I can associate with people a lot of athletes don't like to. I'm a social person: I can talk to anyone."

- "People look at me like their sister. I don't have any negative vibes about me."

- "I'm willing to help others."

- "I'm very respectful of people, a sort of Southern hospitality thing instilled in me by my grandmother."

- "Willingness to do anything for a friend."

- "I make all the players better and enjoy doing it."

- "Ability to get along with all types of people."[6]

There were no references to either winning or toughness, although each of these all-stars had to have demonstrated those qualities to have been selected to the All-USA teams. The New Generation athletes seem to understand that sport allows them to connect with other human beings in meaningful ways. I read these comments by today's athletes as a sign that it will take little persuasion to recruit them as allies in the re-formation of sport. The future looks promising, indeed, for the greening of American sport.

In short, allies are in place, issues upon which to build a common ground are identifiable, and the current climate is right for making changes. Alliances can be forged with those who are invested in the sports enterprise. Not only are athletes and parents served by becoming partners in reform, but also professional sports educators, coaches and athletics administrators, can look to better times when sport adapts to the requirements of the times.

Epilogue

Going for the Gold

Once upon a time in a small kingdom in the Gylanic Mountains there lived a royal family that prided itself in providing all of its subjects with a wide range of opportunities. The queen was a woman who refused to take second position to the king. She worked hard to keep abreast of all manner of issues facing the kingdom.

One day in the early spring one of the kingdom's most able knights returned from an expedition to the mouth of the river that ran through the entire kingdom. He asked for an audience with the king and queen to report what he had discovered. When the king and queen entertained the knight in their quarters, he reported that he had questioned the natives in the wilderness along the river and was told a tale of pirates who had sailed up the river and stashed chests of gold on the river bank. The knight appealed to the king and queen to allow him to assemble an expedition to venture down the river to retrieve the treasure.

That evening the king proposed to the queen that instead of sending the knight they send their son, the prince, as the leader of the expedition. He said, "This would give him a good opportunity to test his manhood and establish himself as a potential leader in the kingdom." The queen responded, "Why not send our daughter, she too needs to be tested so that she can be ready to assume the throne if the circumstances require." The queen would not accept the argument that only men need to be tested and prepared for assuming leadership. After much discussion and argument the king and queen were unable to reach a compromise. Before retiring they pledged to one another that they would work together until they could find a resolution to their differences.

During the night they were visited by a messenger from the gods. The gods were impressed with the willingness of the king and queen to figure out a way for satisfying the needs of both the prince and princess. Through the messenger they commanded the king and queen to hold a festival for all of their subjects where they could celebrate the things that both men and women are able to bring to the kingdom. "During that joyful celebration you will be given signs that will guide your decision," said the messenger. So the king and queen planned the largest Festival that had ever been held and invited representatives from all corners of the kingdom. They were careful not to exclude anyone who wished to join them in the celebration. The celebration included activities for people of all ages. It was clear that the event was uplifting for all of the king's and queen's subjects, for the celebration continued for seven days and seven nights. By the seventh day all of the participants, including the king and queen, were totally exhausted. The members of the royal family were lying in the tall cool grass reflecting upon the joy of the occasion when all of a sudden the skies clouded over and bolts of lighting were followed by loud rounds of thunder. At that moment there appeared in the sky the images of Zeus and Athena, the mighty Greek god and goddess. Together Zeus and his daughter, Athena, commanded the king and queen to seek the counsel of the kingdom's oldest and most trusted wise men and women. The king and queen were assured by Zeus and Athena that they could, indeed, find among their own subjects, the wisdom to resolve this dilemma.

The king and queen invited to the royal court the wisest man and the wisest woman in the kingdom to provide them with the guidance they needed to determine whether to send the prince or the princess in search of the gold. Both the old man and old woman advised the king and queen that each of their children possessed qualities that would serve them well in the search for the buried treasures. "The prince will keep focused on the task and will be strong enough to overcome the difficult barriers to achieving his mission," said the old man. The old woman added, "And the princess will apply her feminine ways to looking after the needs of the crew so that they will be able to endure the hardships of the journey."

After consulting the wise man and wise woman, the king and queen agreed to send both their son and their daughter on separate expeditions. In that way it would be possible to demonstrate whether or not they were ready to chart the course of the kingdom during the years ahead.

In order to permit the princess to assemble a group of women to accompany her on the trip it was necessary for the king and queen to change the laws of the land that prohibited women from risking themselves on such adventures. They proclaimed, "Women will be given the same opportunities as men to seek treasures." This was added to the Book of Covenants of the Kingdom as the 9th Rule of Law.

After re-writing their laws to permit their daughter's crew to risk themselves in jobs that had traditionally been assumed by men, the king and queen called the prince and princess to their chambers to announce their decision. "We are inviting you both to lead expeditions in search of treasures that we have heard are buried on the banks of the river in the wilderness," the king announced. "And we are offering each of you the opportunity to select a crew to join with you on these two separate expeditions. We are confident that both of you possess the capabilities to be successful on this mission," the queen said. "This is not a competition, but an opportunity for the two of you to discover within yourselves those qualities that will allow you to be successful as leaders of the people of our kingdom," the king emphasized.

The prince gathered together the strongest and most adventuresome young warriors to serve on the crew of his sleek racing boat. He taught his crew to travel down the river at great speed and with undivided attention to their goal. During training, any warriors who were not up to the task were quickly replaced with more sturdy young men. The training was rigorous and demanding, for the prince was dedicated to "passing his test."

The princess, on the other hand, assembled a group of her good friends to serve as her crew, expecting that they would be able to develop the skills to become contributors to the expedition. After choosing a canoe for her trip down the river she gathered together her crew. They not only trained together for the expedition, but also had endless sessions discussing how they were going to proceed, making sure that the voice of each crew member was heard. For the princess it was most important that the crew get along with one another. She wanted everyone to be happy, so she listened carefully to the concerns of the crew members and attempted to accommodate the special needs of each. She invited them to be prepared to enjoy the sights as they searched for the treasure.

At the beginning of spring after the river was flowing rapidly with melted snow the two crews launched their boats to begin their adventures down the river toward the sea. A large crowd of the king's and queen's subjects gathered at the dock to bid them good luck, for they all understood clearly that their own destinies were closely tied to the success of their future leaders. This challenge had meaning for all men, women, boys, and girls in the kingdom. Their departure on the adventure became a gala public event. The subjects of the king and queen not only wanted both young people to succeed in their mission so that the kingdom could benefit from the treasure, but they were secretly rooting for the princess to discover the gold, since no other young woman in the history of their kingdom had ever undertaken such a challenge.

Within a few days the prince and his crew returned to report that they had not been successful in finding the treasure. They had been so focused on the goal and on the precision of their stroking, that they failed to see signs of where the treasure had been buried. The prince and his crew were very dispirited and were blaming themselves for letting down the kingdom. They felt like failures for not being able to carry out the king's and queen's orders. They were fearful that they would become targets of public scorn and ridicule for not returning with the gold.

Some time later, the princess and her crew returned. They too were empty-handed, having taken so much time viewing the sights and sharing stories with their crew mates, that by the time they arrived at the wilderness where the treasure was buried the tide had risen, hiding under the water any signs of the pirates' digging. The princess and her crew were also disappointed that they had let down the women of the kingdom for whom they were trying to serve as models. They did report that they felt they were better people for having tried something that no other group of women had ever attempted. Also they were quick to tell stories of the beauty they had encountered along the way. They also believed that they had strengthened their friendships with other members of the crew.

Needless to say, both the king and queen were disappointed that neither of their children had been a successful treasure seeker. Determined not to give up on either the treasure or on the heirs to the thrown, the king and queen again consulted the wise man and wise woman. They said to the king and queen, "It is clear that neither of your children has within himself or herself the characteristics required to meet the challenges lying before them," the wise man reflected. "Unfortunately, the prince has been listening only to the voice of the king and has not developed his full capabilities," observed the wise woman. "And the princess has only been listening to the queen." They advised the king and queen that if the prince and princess were going to be able to develop into the kinds of leaders the kingdom needed for the coming era, it would be necessary for them to learn to listen to both the king's and queen's voices that reside deep inside them. Both the king and queen have something important to teach them.

How were the king and queen going to be able to help their children develop the abilities to seek those treasures that can bring riches to the entire kingdom so that they can exercise their responsibilities to their subjects? The king and queen decided that the best way to help each of their children develop their full potential was to invite them to work together in planning a new expedition that would draw upon each of their personal strengths and the strengths of their crews. It is possible that the male crew members could awaken the voice of the king in the women and the female crew members could strengthen the voice of the queen in the men, so that they could become more complete explorers of the various paths in life. They determined it was worth a try. So this time the king and queen themselves joined with the expedition planners and rewarded crew members each time they allowed the voice of the opposite sex to be expressed. The king and queen said, "We grant you permission to express that side of you that does not generally get expressed." It was not long before both the male and female crew members were sharing with one another their ideas of why they had failed to find the treasure. Very soon, after some difficult times, the two crews were developing a plan for launching their joint expedition in search of the treasure. Within a few months they were ready to christen a new craft they had jointly built that was designed to move at high speeds when needed and to drift from bank to bank when the circumstances required.

The men taught the women how to keep focused on the tasks and not to get distracted by the people around them. And the women taught the men to pay attention to the full range of things going on around them so that they could be more concerned about how they were affecting other members of the crew. The training they experienced together allowed them to develop both their tough and their tender sides, which would serve them well on their river odyssey.

Soon they were on their way down the river paying close attention to how they were going to find the treasure, attending to the beauty of the river banks and the beauty of the reflections in the water of their graceful strokes. They were guided by a sense of responsibility to those loyal men and women at home who held such high hopes for their success. They carefully planned how they would help their fellow boat mates grow through their experiences together. Long before the new crew expected, they spotted evidence of where the treasure had been buried. Lo and behold, they discovered more treasures than they had ever imagined.

When they returned home to the cheering crowd of well-wishers they realized that it was not simply that they had found the gold that made them feel good about themselves, or that they had enriched everyone in the kingdom by their find. They were celebrating because they had learned through their experiences together to give expression to new possibilities. Most importantly they had learned how to listen carefully to both the king's and queen's voices that echoed within their souls, giving them permission to depart from tradition. They were now a more complete new generation who could continue to grow as they worked together to develop a common ground upon which to build their lives together.

References

References

PREFACE
1. Naomi Wolf, *Fire with Fire* (New York: Random House, 1993)
2. Shirley P. Burggraf, *The Feminine Economy & Economic Man* (Reading Massachusetts: Addison-Westley, 1997)
3. Ibid., p. 10
4. Patrick Fanning and Mathew McKay, *Being a Man* (Oakland California: New Harbinger Publications, Inc., 1993) p. 5-6
5. Sam Keen, *Fire in the Belly* (New York: Bantam Books, 1992) p. 10

CHAPTER TWO
1. Charles Reich, *The Greening of America* (New York: Bantam Book, 1970)
2. Sam Keen, Ibid. p. 46
3. Rollo May, *Power and Innocence* (New York: Norton, 1998) p. 54
4. Colin Powell, *My American Journey* (New York: Random House, 1995)
5. Sam Keen, Ibid., p. 153
6. Robert Bork, *Slouching Towards Gomorrah* (New York: Regan Books, 1996) p. 343
7. Warren Farrell, *The Myth of Male Power* (New York: Simon and Schuster,1993) p.42
8. Ibid, p. 44
9. Riane Eisler, *The Chalice and the Blade* (San Francisco: Harper, 1988) p. 121

CHAPTER THREE
1. Christopher Lasch, *The Culture of Narcissism* (New York: Norton, 1979) p. 123

CHAPTER FOUR
1. Sheri Hite, *Women in Love* (New York: St. Martin's Press, 1987) p. 630

CHAPTER FIVE
1. Daphne Rose Kingma, *The Men We Never Knew.* (Berkley/Conari Press, 1993) p.181
2. John Stoltenberg, *Refusing To Be A Man* (New York: Meridian, 1990) p. 188-89
3. Judy Mann, *The Difference* (New York: Warner Books, 1996) p. 282

CHAPTER SIX
1. Michael A. Messner and Donald F. Sabo, *Sex, Violence, and Power in Sports* (Freedom CA: The Crossing Press, 1994) p. 200
2. Kingma, Ibid, p. 239-240

CHAPTER SEVEN
1. Mariah Burton Nelson, *Are We Winning Yet?* (New York: Random House, 1991) p. 9
2. *People Magazine* (Sept. 14, 1992)
3. Sam Keen, Ibid., p. 204

REFERENCES

4. George A. Selleck , *How to Play the Game of Your Life* (South Bend, Indiana: Diamond Communications, 1995)

CHAPTER EIGHT

1. Billy Jean King,*Women's Sports and Fitness*, November-December 1992, p. 79
2. Christopher Lasch, Ibid., p. 103
3. Donna Lopiano, *Christian Science Monitor*, Nov. 6,1992, p.15
4. Digger Philps, *The Associated Press*, Quoted in The NCAA News, January 1994, p. 17
5. Vince Lombardi, Quoted by S.J. Hoffman in *The Chronicle of Higher Education*, Nov. 11, 1992, p. A44
6. Eddie Sefko, *Houston Chronicle*, April 15, 1993, p. C1
7. Fran Blinbury, *Houston Chronicle*, August 30, 1998, p.B1

CHAPTER NINE

1. Stephen Covey, *The 7 Habits of Highly Effective People* (New York: A Fireside Book, 1989), p. 263
2. Ken Burns, *USA Today*, September 13, 1994, p. 13A
3. Naomi Wolf, Ibid., p. 190
4. Riki Robbins Jones *The Empowered Woman* (New York: S.P.I. Books, 1992) p. 190
5. Jackline Light, quoted in Jones, Ibid., p. 194
6. *USA Today*, April 18, 1995, p. 4C and April 20, 1995, p. 10C.